PHILLY HOOPS:

THE SPHAS AND WARRIORS

JAMES ROSIN

James Rosin

PHILLY HOOPS:
THE SPHAS AND WARRIORS

Published by Autumn Road Publishers
Philadelphia, Pennsylvania

Library of Congress Control Number: 2003090565

ISBN 0-9728684-0-2

Printed by George H Buchanan, Bridgeport, NJ

TABLE OF CONTENTS

James Rosin grew up in Philadelphia and graduated from Temple University's School of Communications and the Theater. In New York he studied acting with Bobby Lewis and appeared in plays off-off Broadway, and did Summer Stock in New England. In Hollywood, he played featured roles in twenty-three network television shows. As a writer, his first full-length play was produced by theater companies in New York and Los Angeles. He also wrote stories and teleplays for three network television series. His one-hour documentary Philly Hoops: The SPHAS and Warriors has aired on public television.

AUTHOR'S NOTE

This book was compiled from historical facts, statistics, and information in the public domain. It was supplemented by interviews with former players from both teams as well as those associated with both organizations.

Philly Hoops is Dedicated to:

Paul Arizin

Gil Fitch

Tom Gola

Red Klotz

Harvey Pollack

ACKNOWLEDGMENTS

I would like to thank the fine people who helped me to create the content of this book: Paul Arizin, Gil Fitch, Tom Gola, Red Klotz, Harvey Pollack, Jerry Rullo, Angelo Musi, Frank Washington, George Dempsey, Ernie Beck, Al Shrier, Ron Avery, Simcha Gersh, Al Attles, Jerry Fleishman and Bill Campbell.

Also, Margaret Jerrido, Brenda Wright, Evan Towle, Urban Archives, Temple University Library; Sloan Millstein, Philadelphia Jewish Sports Hall of Fame; Marvin Black, Mickey Black; Leaden Bernstein; Ron Pollack; Don Davis, Philadelphia Jewish Archives Center; Clem Murray, Philadelphia Inquirer; Michael Mercanti, Philadelphia Daily News; Ed Voves, Philadelphia Inquirer–Daily News Research Library; The Jewish Exponent; Naismith Memorial Basketball Hall of Fame, Hoop Hall of Fame.com and The Golden State Warriors.

FOREWORD

The SPHAS and the Warriors were the first two professional basketball teams in the City of Philadelphia. Both franchises were owned and operated by Eddie Gottlieb, "the mogul of basketball." The Philadelphia SPHAS played professionally from 1918 until the birth of the National Basketball Association in 1949. In 1946, Gottlieb formed the Philadelphia Warriors who would compete first in the Basketball Association of America, from 1946-49, then in the NBA from 1949 until 1962 when the team was sold and the franchise relocated to San Francisco. That spanned a 44-year period in Philadelphia sports history.

It was interesting to meet and talk with the pro basketball players from my childhood, who lifted my spirits and allowed me to soar to the basket. As I listened to them reflect on a time that was, it made me realize how much of our past enriches our future. Enjoy the journey back!

THE PHILADELPHIA SPHAS
1918-1954

In the early 1900s thousands of Eastern European Jews flocked to America and settled in eastern cities like New York and Philadelphia in search of a better tomorrow. Many of the new arrivals were tradesmen, merchants and skilled workers. They needed to be in a city to find jobs, and many settled in South Philadelphia because that's where the ship docked. Everyone was equal, in the same predicament, and struggled to make a living.

Italians, Irish, Polish, Jewish, and Afro-Americans all learned to live together. With 54 houses on a street and 80 kids on a block, it wasn't uncommon to find a peach basket on every phone pole.

LEADEN BERNSTEIN
(JEWISH BASKETBALL LEAGUE
1933-41)

> The nice thing about basketball was you could play by yourself. You didn't need anybody else. You needed a ball. That was it. And you could go out and play for hours. Eventually, other kids would come along and join in.

In the beginning, basketball had earned a notorious reputation. The rules provided for few fouls, making the game a barely-controlled melee. There were no out-of-bounds and many courts were ringed with chicken wire, then steel mesh, to keep the ball from hitting spectators.

It was common practice to drive your man into the wire and pile-ups were as frequent as at football games today. Injured players paraded on and off the court with bandaged legs and bleeding heads. Eventually, a rope net was substituted for the metal cage. However, the game was banned at the YMCA.

But the varsity team at South Philadelphia High School introduced a different style of play.

Eddie Gottlieb, Harry Passon, Edwin "Hughie" Black, Mockie Bunin and Charles Neuman, all sons of Jewish immigrants, led Southern to City titles in 1914, 1915 and 1916. That championship team played a quick passing and running style of game. They say it was really something to see the way they moved the ball around. This was opposed to the bullying and fighting way which was so popular other places.

Eddie Gottlieb was originally born in Kiev, Ukraine. His parents brought him to the United States when he was a young child, and Gottlieb was involved with basketball for most of the rest of his life. In 1910, at the age of 12, he began playing with the Combine Club, a group of Jewish grade school boys. Many of them later played for South Philadelphia High School. Gottlieb had an overpowering objective in life after high school . . . to study basketball. His first step was to organize a semi-professional basketball team, along with Hughie Black and Harry Passon, which began in 1917 as an amateur group under the banner of the YMHA.

When the YMHA withdrew its sponsorship, the team sought a new home. At 4th and Reed was a social club called the South Philadelphia Hebrew Association. Some of its members were athletically inclined and they knew Gottlieb and company from South Philly High. So in 1918 the organization agreed to buy uniforms with its initials and the Mogen David as team symbols. The team broke away from the Y and began playing under the auspices of the South Phila. Hebrew Association where it got the name it would carry for the next 36 years.

Eddie Gottlieb became coach and Hughie Black was made Captain. Beside the three founding members were Charlie Neuman, Mockie Bunin, Chickie Passon, Harry's younger brother, and Lou Schneiderman.

The games were low scoring and defensive with faking, two-hand dribbling and passing. The ball was larger than today's, and the rules were different. They would toss the ball at center court after each score. And all the shots were made two-handed with both feet on the ground. The ball was leather-covered with a bladder that was laced inside, and an inflation tube that protruded. It lasted about two years with occasional aid from the shoemaker when there was a tear or when it started getting scuffed up.

Passon, Gottlieb and Black started a sporting goods store called PGB so they could order new uniforms wholesale.

While Gottlieb and Black went to Normal School, Philadelphia's teachers' college, Harry Passon devoted more time to the store which eventually became his and was renamed Passon's Sporting Goods. But Gottlieb always kept an office upstairs. Passon and Black turned over their shares of the team to Gottlieb, who became the sole owner.

Through the early to mid-twenties, the SPHAS played in a small grouping called the Philadelphia League, won two consecutive championships, then joined the Eastern League. They played their games on auditorium stages, ballroom floors, and sometimes in gymnasium cages.

The pay was 5 to 10 dollars a game and Eddie Gottlieb would hand out the money in cash. With wages that low, nobody depended on basketball for his livelihood. So all the SPHAS players had weekday jobs as teachers, mailmen, lawyers and salesmen. One player was a violinist.

By 1926 the SPHAS were known as one of the highest scoring teams of that era. Against Hammonton, identified in the papers as New Jersey Champions, they won by a score of 75-11. When the Eastern League disbanded, it forced the SPHAS to book their own exhibition games.

Fortunately, Gottlieb was a shrewd entrepreneur and up to the task. He used his contacts to set up a series of exhibition games against teams from New York's Metropolitan League and the far-reaching American Basketball League which had just begun operation. The SPHAS won five of six games, losing only to the ABL's premier team, the Cleveland Rosenblums. So

Gottlieb arranged for a best of 3 series against both the original Celtics, and New York Rens. The SPHAS defeated the Rens 2-0, and the Celtics 2-1. Within six weeks, Gottlieb's team had won 9 out of 11 games against some of the most celebrated squads in professional basketball.

By the end of the 1926 season the SPHAS became inactive. Many of the players went on to other pursuits that paid regular wages. That same year a Philadelphia franchise was started by a man named Max Hoff in the ABL. Hoff called his team the Philadelphia Warriors and employed Gottlieb as coach. Gottlieb hired a couple of ex-SPHAS: Lou Schneiderman and Chickie Passon. The Warriors lasted two seasons and then the new league fell apart. It was said the owners couldn't handle the high costs of travel and hotels.

Gottlieb began to promote boxing matches and would also rent Shibe Park or even Yankee Stadium to book black baseball teams to compete against each other. Later he became owner of the Philadelphia Stars that played in the Negro Leagues from 1936 to 1950, and he did scheduling for all the League's games.

Eddie Gottlieb, known to his friends and players as "Gotty," did it all. He was a founder, owner, coach, player, administrator, promoter and became the "mogul of basketball." He always had something up his sleeve. He was a canny businessman and a colorful personality. And he knew the game of basketball inside and out. He had a great mind, like a computer, and his memory was almost faultless. He remembered the scores of games, gate receipts, attendance, and even the weather that day. He loved to win and hated to lose.

SIMCHA GERSH
(PRESIDENT, JEWISH BASKETBALL LEAGUE ALUMNI)

> One night the SPHAS lost an out-of-town game that they should have won, and Eddie thought the team let him down. After the game, he went into a drug store, bought a bottle of iodine and poured it all over the back of his shirt. So they're all eating in a restaurant, Eddie stands up, takes his shirt off, turns around and says, "You guys stabbed me in the back."

A sportswriter once wrote: "During the game when things weren't going well, Gotty would sit on the bench and suffer. He would yank at his tie, gaze upward for divine intervention, bury his face in his hands, and bellow louder than a bull when an official made a questionable call. He loved to win and would instill that in his players. He was tough, yet whenever they spoke of him, it was with respect and admiration."

JERRY FLEISHMAN
(SPHAS 1943-45; PHILADELPHIA WARRIORS 1946-50, 1952-53)

> Whenever Gotty spoke to you, he would keep talking 'til he ran out of air. He always worked to squeeze the last word out. He had all this energy and he couldn't wait until he got it out.

BILL CAMPBELL
(RADIO & TV BROADCASTER)

The mogul kind of looked on Jerry Fleishman as a son. Jerry played for him as a SPHA and a Warrior for about 8 seasons. But Jerry was always in Gotty's doghouse. For one thing or another. No matter what happened, it was always Jerry's fault. Well, one night I'm broadcasting a game, a bad pass is thrown, and Gotty jumps up and starts screaming, "Jerry-you-this" and "Jerry-you-that." The problem was someone forgot to tell Gotty that Jerry Fleishman was seated on the bench two seats away from me.

In 1929 Gottlieb reorganized the SPHAS and recruited college stars to fill his roster. That same year the SPHAS joined the third edition of the old Eastern League and competed against teams from Philadelphia, Reading, Trenton, Camden, and Wilmington. The SPHAS won three championships and narrowly lost a fourth to the Trenton Moose in the 1933 playoffs.

A local player who joined the revamped SPHAS was Harry Litwack, a powerful left-handed shooter and two-time Captain of Temple University's basketball team. Litwack played seven seasons with the SPHAS and helped them capture championships in both the Eastern and American Basketball Leagues. He later coached the SPHAS, became head coach at Temple and had only one losing season in 26 years of coaching.

What made Litwack legendary in Philadelphia was his flawless character. He had a wonderful ability to handle and coach college players, and he had outstanding sportsmanship. He had only one technical foul in 26 years as coach of the freshman and varsity teams.

AL SHRIER
(SPORTS INFORMATION DIRECTOR, TEMPLE UNIVERSITY)

Harry Litwack, one of the all-time great people in the world. Everyone adored him. His former players would come back to see him time and again. He was a teacher, educator, father and friend, besides being an unbelievable coach. He did it all for the sport of basketball and we were very fortunate to have had someone like him.

BERNSTEIN

Another standout was Cy Kaselman. He was also from South Philly. Cy was quiet and handsome. His nickname was "Sundodger" 'cause he played all night and slept all day.

FRANK WASHINGTON
(PHILADELPHIA GIANTS 1941
N.Y. RENS-WASHINGTON BEARS 1945,
HARLEM GLOBETROTTERS 1947-1960)

Cy Kaselman was a pure shooter who never played high school or college ball. Yet he had one of the greatest set-shots I ever saw. Just about everything he shot were rainbows from half-court and he made 'em.

Other notable players in that decade were: forward Gil Fitch, a gifted athlete who had captained Temple's basketball, baseball and soccer teams in 1932; guard Inky Lautman from Central High School, versatile and ambidextrous under the basket; forward Red Rosan, smart, tenacious and one of Temple

University's first All-Americans; Red Wolfe, an inspired and relentless New Yorker who shot underhanded; Shikey Gotthofer, another New Yorker who was stocky, broad shouldered, tough, and knew how to move the ball; and Moe Goldman, an athletic center, from CCNY. And don't forget Dave Zinkoff.

Dave Zinkoff, a native Philadelphian and Temple University grad, first wrote publicity for the SPHAS and did promotions. He would hand out a salami before each game that came from his father's delicatessen at 40th and Girard. And there was always the lucky number in one of the programs. The winner got a $19.95 suit from Sam Gerson's store at 6th and Bainbridge. Then Dave became the public address announcer. On road trips he was sort of a team mascot. Gottlieb would drive the team's eight-seat Ford touring car, the seven members of his squad would sit and Zink would stretch out on the floor between the seats.

GERSH

> When Zink first auditioned for the job, he went to Eddie's office at 5th and Market. So Eddie says, "Stand over there and say 40 words." So Zink does. Then Eddie says, "Face the wall and say 40 words." By this time Zink thinks Eddie is meshuga. But he gives Zink the job. After a while, Zink tells Eddie he wants a raise. He's making five dollars a week and he wants six. Why? Because he's doing a good job and people are coming to see him. So Eddie says, "Let's see." So he fires Zink, gets a new announcer and gives Zink a job handing out programs. After two weeks, Zink can't stand it anymore and asks for his old job back. So Eddie looks around at the full house and says, "It doesn't

GERSH (Cont'd)

look like we lost any customers." But Zink gets his job back and a week later six dollars shows up in his pay envelope.

In 1933, the SPHAS were invited to join the newly-reorganized American Basketball League and remained there. Mostly all of the franchises were located within driving distance of each other in the northeast, with games played in small arenas, armories and dance halls.

GERSH

One day, they were driving to Reading in a really bad storm and the roads were icy. Eddie lost control of the car, it went into a ditch and overturned. He climbed out, turned to his players and said, "Gentlemen, we all go our separate ways. But make sure you're at the game tonight." The team had to thumb rides but made it back to Philadelphia in time for the game.

Premier teams in the League were the Brooklyn Visitations, the last champions of the ABL, and an outstanding St. John's team who had amassed a 70-4 record in three years of college and remained intact as the New York Jewels. But it was the SPHAS who dominated.

By the 1930s, many steps had been taken to advance professional basketball. Exclusive player contracts were required, roster jumping was outlawed, standard-size backboards were mandatory, two-handed dribbling was banned, and caged courts were eliminated. In 1932 the three-second rule limiting time in the lane was introduced and in 1937 the center jump after every basket was eliminated.

The SPHAS went on to win seven titles in thirteen seasons and twice were runners-up. At the height of their success, the SPHAS were one of the best teams in the country, sweeping league games and challenging teams in other cities.

By this time, the game had spread westward to Cleveland and Chicago. However, with travel costly, the chief rivals, in addition to the Visitations and Jewels, were in New York: the Holman-coached Hakoahs, the Celtics, a powerful Jewish-Irish team, the Knights of St. Anthony which represented the mixed Italian and Jewish Brooklyn neighborhood of Greenpoint, and the New York Renaissance, the premier black team who played for 27 seasons and won over 2500 games.

WASHINGTON

> The New York Renaissance was also known as the New York Rens. They were named after the Harlem Renaissance Ballroom, their home court, and had some great Philadelphia players. Tarzan Cooper from Central High School, was the toughest center I ever saw. About 6'6" and 280 pounds, with arms down to his knees, he would stand in the hole and players would fall off him like water off a duck. You couldn't move him. If you brought a trailer and ran it into Tarzan, you'd hurt the trailer. Zach Clayton was from Gratz and one of the greatest all-around athletes Philly had. He could do everything. He later became the first black referee in professional boxing. There was Jackie Bethard, a mentor to many young players, and Bill Yancy.

The New York Rens introduced a style of play based on speed, crisp passes and relentless defense. On the road, the team was often refused lodging and food. Sometimes they were forced to drive 200 miles to play a game. But despite the racism they faced, the Rens overcame it and became a great team.

FLEISHMAN

We were never able to beat the Rens on their home court. But one time we were up by five points with about 20 seconds to go. They had glass backboards attached to cables up in the balcony. Every time we shot the ball, their fans would pull on the cables and the backboards would move. The last 20 seconds of that game lasted about 5 minutes. But we finally won by one point.

Racial intolerance and bigotry were not alone. Religious discrimination was pervasive and escalated in the 1930s. American Jewish people were barred from many professions and schools, and anti-Semitic broadcasts were aired every Sunday. While Hitler enacted anti-Jewish laws and set up concentration camps, the German-American Bund in Philadelphia wore Nazi uniforms, paraded and held anti-Jewish rallies.

Gottlieb's answer: The SPHAS would be the best team in basketball and, at the same time, not hide their identity.

MARVIN BLACK
(SON OF HUGHIE BLACK)

In the 1930s the players came onto the court wearing these very flashy warm-up outfits — fancy mackinaws and jackets, and they'd remove them at the last minute to reveal their uniforms with the

BLACK (Cont'd)

initials: Samech, Pey, Hey, Aleph and a Jewish star. The uniforms in those days were basically tight-fitting jerseys, plaid shorts, knee pads, long socks, and high-top shoes.

GIL FITCH
(SPHAS FORWARD, 1932-39)

We played about four games a week, usually two league games and exhibition games against teams from Scranton, Wilkes Barre, Pittsburgh, Chicago and Oshkosh, Wisconsin. The season began in early November and ran until sometime in April.

The SPHAS won all of their games in the spring of 1934 and went on to win the play-offs their first year. They dominated the American League, winning titles in 1934, 1936, 1937, 1939, 1940, 1943 and 1945. When they didn't win the title, they led the league in scoring.

But sometimes things got difficult. And it wasn't just the slurs and biased officials. One night in Jersey City, Harry Litwack went after a ball out of bounds, a fan grabbed it, and wouldn't give it back. So Harry took it. At half-time someone hit Harry over the head with a Coke bottle and, before you knew it, Eddie, Harry and the remaining five players were trading punches with an angry mob. The police had to escort them out and Harry was taken to the hospital.

Another time against the Brooklyn Visitations in New York, Shikey Gotthofer had the ball on the sidelines ready to in-bound. A fan took a lit cigar and jammed it into Shikey's thigh.

Shikey almost jumped into the balcony, except there were fans up there dropping bags of wet sand on the team. Talk about spectator involvement.

Things were more peaceful back in Philadelphia. In the early 1930s, the SPHAS began to play their home games at the Broadwood Hotel and it became quite a social event.

RED KLOTZ
(SPHAS 1942-43, 1945-48, 1949-51)

> The Broadwood Hotel had a beautiful grand ballroom with stage, balcony, and a dance floor large enough for a basketball court. So every Saturday night, Gotty would sell out. About 1500 people — 65 cents for men, 35 cents for women. Gil Fitch, one of our players, had a band. So after each game, he'd rush out, shower, change, climb on the stage, and become band leader for the dance that followed. Singer Kitty Kallen got her start there. It was a wonderful social event and a place where men would meet their girlfriends. People would dress immaculately. Even the young kids wore suits. Women were dressed in their finest to impress. How many met at the SPHAS games is anyone's guess. Scores of Philadelphians have probably told their grandchildren about how Grandpop and Grandmom met at a basketball game at a Broad Street hotel.

FITCH

> I always loved music and began playing the alto saxophone at age 11. When I turned 14, I quit school and toured with the Major Revue, a wonderful group of talented child performers. After 8 months, I decided to go back to Central High School. But my music never left me. After

FITCH (Cont'd)

graduating from Central High, I went to Temple U on an athletic scholarship in 1928. By 1932, my senior year, I was captain of the basketball, baseball and soccer teams. In September of that year Eddie Gottlieb asked me if I would play for the SPHAS. Four years after I joined the SPHAS, in 1936, I told Gotty I was going to form a band. He liked the idea and suggested we play after each Saturday night game at the Broadwood Hotel. It boosted ticket sales and packed the house. It was a great social evening. At the same time, I needed a songstress. I heard Kitty Kallen on the Kiddy Hour at WCAU. What a voice she had. So at age 15 she came to sing with us. Her mother wouldn't allow her to come to the Broadwood by herself. So I always picked her up and took her home. The band became very popular and we began to play at the Bellevue Stratford and other major hotels in the Philadelphia area. By 1939, I had so many bookings, I decided to devote full time to the band and my music.

There were double and triple-headers at Convention Hall, and the SPHAS would play away games in places like New York, Trenton, Paterson or Elizabeth, usually in an armory. They played about 55 games a season with a short play-off series.

KLOTZ

It was a much different game then. We played under the basket. Today they play over it. We played fundamentals. We passed the ball, moved very quickly, and played defense. It was a team game. Not everyone wanted to shoot. Usually guards were good outside shooters, and never missed their foul shots. Our forwards would run their men off a pick or a cut, and we'd get them the

KLOTZ (Cont'd)

ball. When you didn't hit the open man or took a bad shot, you'd have to explain yourself. If you didn't have a good explanation, you'd be on the bench. Centers usually didn't handle the ball or shoot much. Their job was to rebound, although we had a very good center in Moe Goldman who had a great left-handed hook. We had a lot of fun playing together and we were all very close.

Probably no one ever logged more miles and minutes on the basketball court than Red Klotz. After graduating from South Philadelphia High and two years of play at Villanova, Klotz joined the SPHAS in 1942 and played with fellow South Philadelphian Petey Rosenberg, known for his great moves and beautiful hook shot, and Chink Morganstine, a strong front-line player, from Temple. During the war years, from 1942 on, their teammates included a new group of mostly New Yorkers: Irv Davis, guard Ozzie Schectman, Ralph Kaplowitz, another guard with great moves, Butch Schwartz, a smart team player; centers Art Hillhouse, Irv Rothenberg, and forwards Len and Howie Radar, all from LIU, forward Dutch Garfinkle, a great assist man who initiated the no-look pass, center-forward Irv Torgoff, a good rebounder, and forward Jerry Fleishman, a versatile All American from NYU whom Eddie Gottlieb signed as a sophomore in 1943.

FLEISHMAN

When Eddie asked me to play for the SPHAS I was taken by the army. Fortunately, I was stationed at Fort Jackson in South Carolina so every weekend I'd take the train into Philadelphia. After our

FLEISHMAN (Cont'd)

Saturday night game at the Broadwood, we'd drive down to Wilmington on Sunday afternoon and play the Bombers. Then we'd rush out, without even taking a shower, and drive north to play the Trenton Tigers or Paterson Crescents. We had no ownership deals or player contracts in those days. You played according to the deal you had with the promoter. If he had a bad turnout due to weather, he'd pay you less. Generally we made a hundred bucks per game if the house was good.

After two years in the Air Force, Klotz rejoined the team. In 1946, he coached them for a series and defeated the Harlem Globetrotters.

The Globetrotters were formed in 1927 by Abe Saperstein. They were originally called the "Savoy Five" and operated out of Chicago. They gave their audience much to marvel at and laugh about at the same time. Behind players Sweetwater Clifton, "Goose" Tatum, Ermer Robinson, Marcus Haines, Ducky Moore, Boyd Buie, and Frank Washington, they were a star attraction all over the United States.

After playing one year with the 1947 Baltimore Bullets in the newly-formed B.A.A. and winning a championship, Klotz went back to coaching.

In 1949 he rejoined the SPHAS as a player-coach. Abe Saperstein never forgot his loss to the SPHAS, or Red Klotz either.

Respecting Klotz's skill and competitive nature, Saperstein offered him a unique opportunity: form his own team and tour with the Globetrotters. Klotz took him up on it and in 1952 formed the Washington Generals. Klotz toured with the Globetrotters all over the world. He coached and played until he was 62, and to this day remains owner-general manager of the same organization now known as the New York Nationals.

He helped to make basketball an international sport by pioneering the game. In 50 years he played, coached and gave clinics all over the world, in over 110 countries, before kings, queens and Popes. At one time, when you went overseas, all you saw were soccer balls. Now you see basketballs. And many of the young players that have come out of Europe are a result of that. The basketball gods have looked down on Red Klotz and nodded in solemn approval.

CAMPBELL

> On a Globetrotters tour in Rome before the Pope, Red was concerned that the "Sweet Georgia Brown" theme during warmups might not be appropriate in the presence of the holy leader. But when they played it, Red's concerns were put to rest. He looked up and saw the Pope's left foot keeping time with the music.

In the mid-1940s, the new generation of Jews began moving out to the suburbs and on to other pursuits. Dominion over the urban basketball courts began to pass to the Afro-American who was migrating north from dying southern farms in search of opportunity and a future for his children.

By 1946 the SPHAS and American Basketball League had seen its day as the top professional basketball team and league, with the emergence of the Basketball Association of America and the Philadelphia Warriors as the premier team. But the SPHAS continued to compete in the ABL against teams in Wilmington, Jersey City, Elizabeth, Paterson, Trenton, Brooklyn, Hartford, Wilkes Barre, and Scranton.

FRANK STANCZAK
(SPHAS GUARD, 1948-49)

During the war years, most of the SPHAS team was made up of New York players. But in the late 1940s, our line-up was mostly Philadelphians who were high school stars in the City's public league: Stan Brown, Len Weiner, Aaron Tanitsky, Bill McCahan, Mendy Snyder and Eddie Lyons.

EDDIE LYONS
(SPHAS GUARD, 1947-49)

We played 34 league games a season in the post-war ABL. Half of our home games were played as a preliminary event to the Warriors at the Arena. The remainder of our home games were played at the Broadwood. Most of our away games were played in armories, and in places like Wilkes Barre, Trenton and Hartford we drew big crowds. I got paid about 50 dollars a game and for some reason the bigger guys got paid about $60. Harry Litwack was our coach and both he and Gotty were very good to us. When I tore up my knee in a game against the Jersey City Atoms, Gotty made sure I had the best orthopedic surgeon in Philly. He paid

LYONS (Cont'd)

all my medical expenses and compensated me for the games I missed. I came back the next season and played in every game.

In 1949, a depleted SPHAS group dropped out of the ABL and became an exhibition team. When Red Klotz returned as player-coach, he staged exhibition games with the Harlem Globetrotters all across the country.

In 1952, Pete Monska succeeded Klotz as coach.

BOB LOJEWSKI
(SPHAS FORWARD, 1952-54)

When I joined the SPHAS in '52, there were three exhibition teams that played the Globetrotters. The other two were the Washington Generals and Toledo Mercuries. We played about 8 games a week and on the weekends we played both afternoon and evening games. I played my first SPHA game in Madison Square Garden. I was about 19, could jump over the roof, but knew nothing about the Globetrotters or their style of play. They put me on "Goose" Tatum, and the first time he tried his patented hook shot, I blocked it. He tried it again and I blocked that too. So he turned and spit at me. I was shocked. I couldn't believe it. Here was this established star and he couldn't take the heat. At the time-out, Pete (Monska) instructed me to give him more room. But Pete wasn't too upset about it. I think he got pleasure out of watching "Goose" Tatum get his shot stuffed.

GEORGE DEMPSEY
(SPHAS GUARD, 1951-52)

When I would cover "Goose" in the pivot, he did this act where he would place the ball on the floor, pretend to look for it, and we were supposed to go along with the act and pretend to look for it too. But I never pretended. The minute I saw the loose ball, I would pick it up and dribble down the floor with it, and that would ruin their act. After I did it a few times, Abe Saperstein told Pete Monska I had to go along with the act or I was off the tour. All in all, it was a great experience playing with the SPHAS during their exhibition years. I got to travel all over the country, was paid well, and it turned out to be a stepping-stone to the NBA.

In 1954, the SPHAS disbanded. The little team that couldn't but did survived for 36 years, and left a rich legacy in Philadelphia sports history.

Edwin "Hughie" Black, Captain and Cofounder of the original 1918 SPHAS. He later became Assistant Coach and remained with the team through their championship years in the Eastern League (1929-1931). Hughie and his wife Selma then created Pine Forest Camp in the Poconos which still remains in operation today.

THE SPHAS

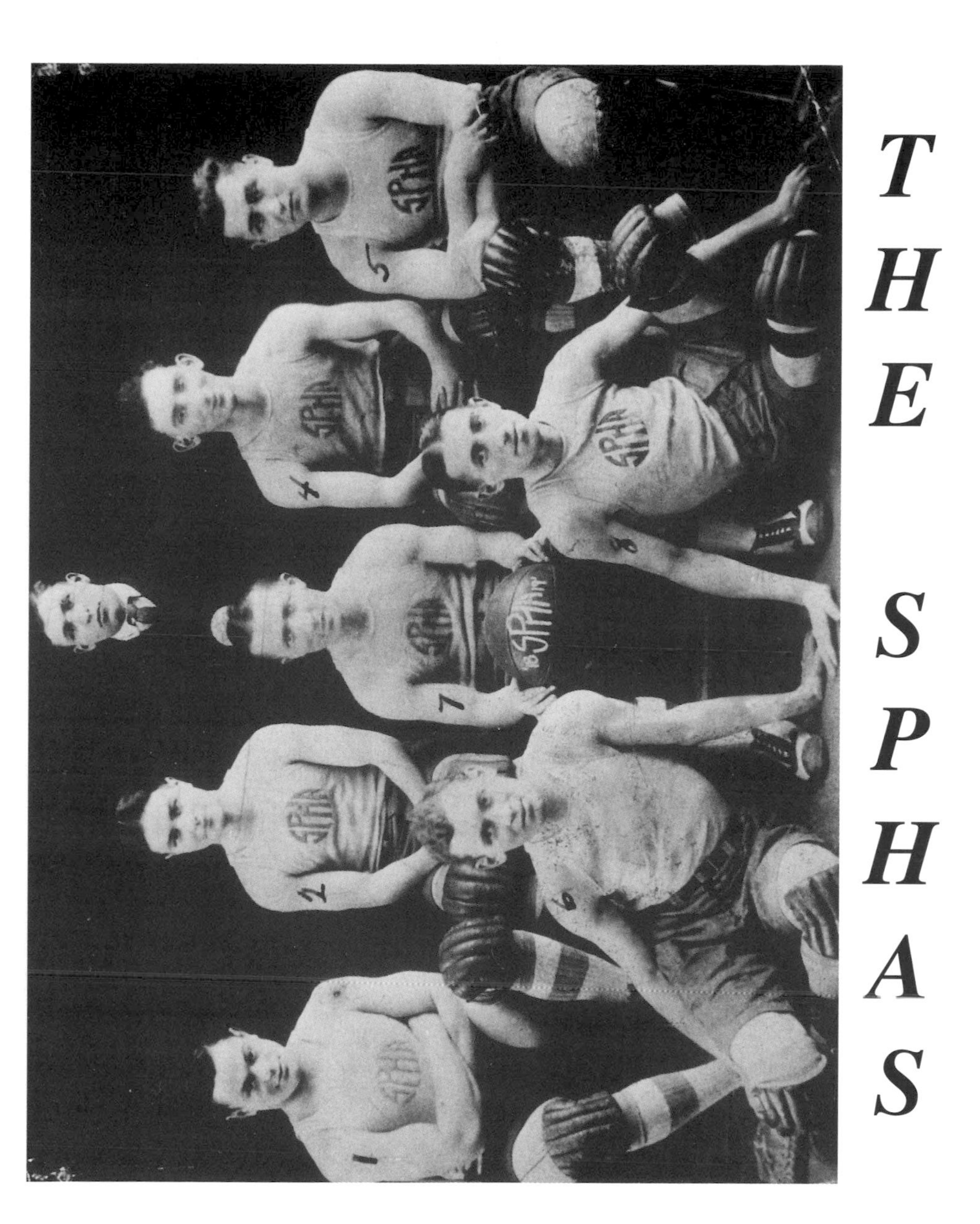

1918–1954

The original SPHAS team in 1918. L to R: Charlie Neuman, Mockie Bunin, Hughie Black (holding ball), Chicky Passon, and Eddie Gottlieb. Bottom row: Harry Passon and Lou Schneiderman.

The SPHAS: Eastern League Champions 1929-31.

PHILADELPHIA HEBREWS – SPHAS

The 1933 SPHAS team in the American League. L to R: Eddie Gottlieb, Harry Litwack, Red Wolfe, Inky Lautman, Lou Forman, Gil Fitch, Shikey Gotthofer, Cy Kaselman. (Philadelphia Jewish Archives)

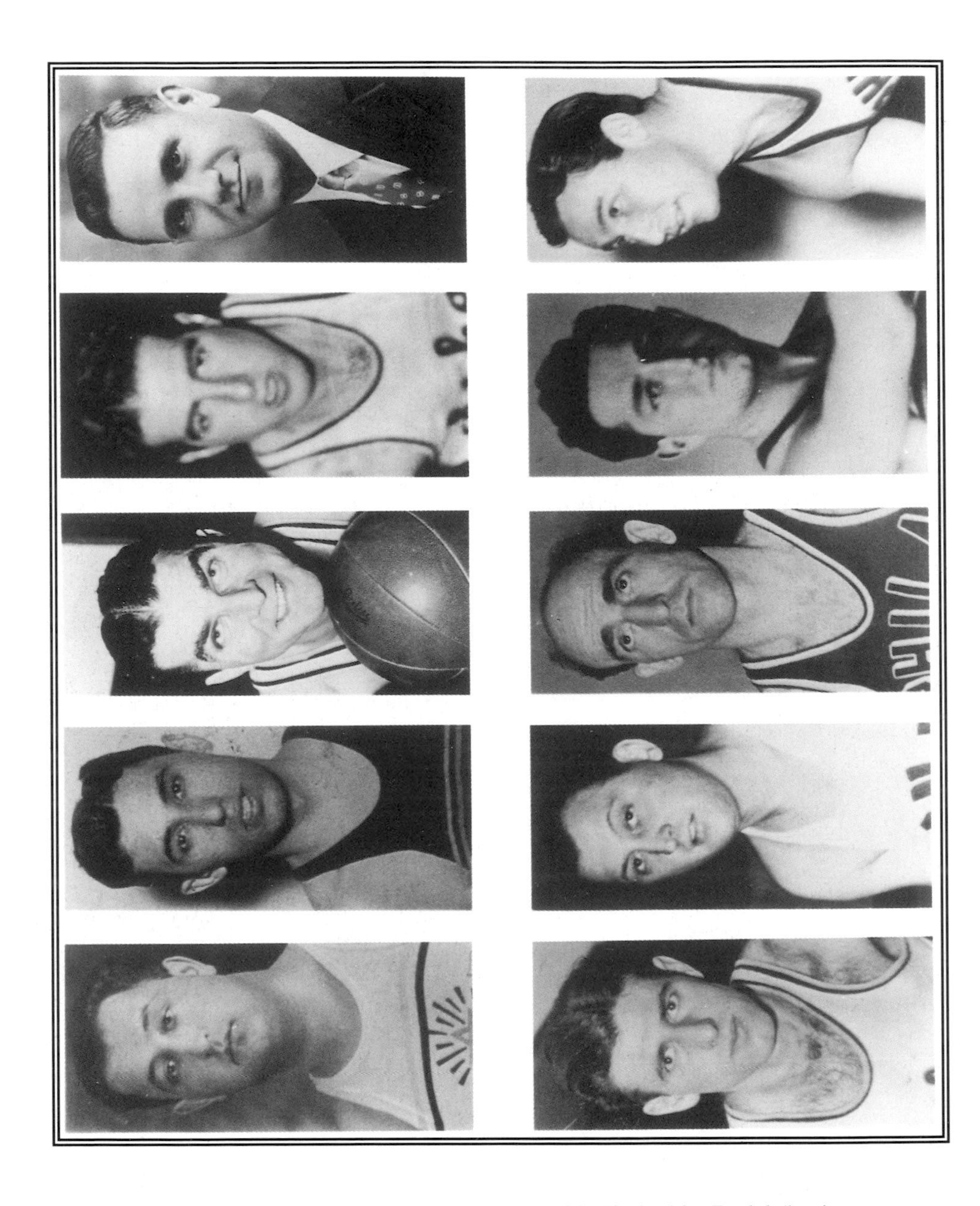

Top: Eddie Gottlieb, Lou Forman, Cy Kaselman, Gil Fitch, Abe Radel (business manger). Bottom row: Moe Goldman, Inky Lautman, Red Wolfe, Harry Litwack, Shikey Gotthofer. (Philadelphia Jewish Archives)

The SPHAS 1936-37 ABL Champions.

Gil Fitch, a three-letter man at Temple University who captained the basketball, baseball and soccer teams. He played for the SPHAS from 1932-39 and was also an accomplished musician and well-known band leader.

Petey Rosenberg from South Philadelphia joined the SPHAS for the 1938-39 season. He later played for the Warriors during the 1946-47 season.

The SPHAS in April 1940. Most of the 1930's cast would be gone after winning the championship in 1943. (Philadelphia Jewish Archives)

Red Klotz as a SPHAS player in 1942.

Red Klotz as a player-coach in 1949. SPHAS vs. Globetrotters at the Olympic Auditorium in Los Angeles.

The Harlem Globetrotters in 1948. Top row: Louis "Babe" Pressley, Frank Washington, Nat "Sweetwater" Clifton, William "Pop" Gates, Reece "Goose" Tatem. Bottom row: Ermer Robinson, Ducky Moore, Marcus Haines, and Boyd Buie.

Frank Washington (1950s).

Ready for an overseas Globetrotter tour in the mid 1950s. Front row: Abe Saperstein, Red Klotz, Eddie Gottlieb, Dave Zinkoff. Back row: Cy Kaselman, Rookie Brown, and Frank Washington.

Dave Zinkoff in 1948.

Sphas Sparks

VOL. 6 — No. 2 SATURDAY, NOVEMBER 6, 1943 PHILA., PA.

Trenton Invades Broadwood For League Opening Next Sat., Nov. 13 Continuing Last Season's Thrillers

"INKY" LAUTMAN

Still young in years, Inky is starting his eleventh season as a Sphas regular. His tricky shooting ability has always made him a valuable ace, difficult for the opposition to stop. Has been a main cog on all six championship teams, and is expected to play important role in current loop race.

The thrills of last season's championship playoff games will be resumed here next Saturday, November 13, when the Trenton Tigers appear on the Broadwood Hotel Ballroom court to help Eddie Gottlieb's Sphas open their current American League campaign.

Fans will long remember the close and sensational seven-game series. How each team upset the dope, winning on their opponent's court, until the final game here. Then, with the gun ready to end the second period, the Sphas were sparked by the never to be forgotten 70-foot one-hand shot of Irv Torgoff, pulling the game out of the fire, thus finally winning the championship, after a brilliantly played and stubbornly fought series, that brought the rivalry of these two teams to its highest pitch.

The five Trenton regulars will all be back next Saturday. Ace Goldstein, Mike Bloom, Matt Guokas, Herb Gershon, Dick Fitzgerald, aided by outstanding newcomers, will be thirsting for revenge!

Sellout crowds are on hand when the Sphas play Trenton. Get choice seats by ordering early. In fact, we suggest that you follow the example of many others, and make reservations for every home game.

PRIZE DRAWING NUMBER

Nº 441

Compliments of
Sam Gerson and Jackie Gordon

TICKETS

Reserve Early by Phoning
LOMbard 4808 or **5893**
Or Calling at
PASSON'S, 509 MARKET STREET
Reservations Will Be Held Until
9 P. M. Unless Otherwise Requested

A SPHAS program from 1943.

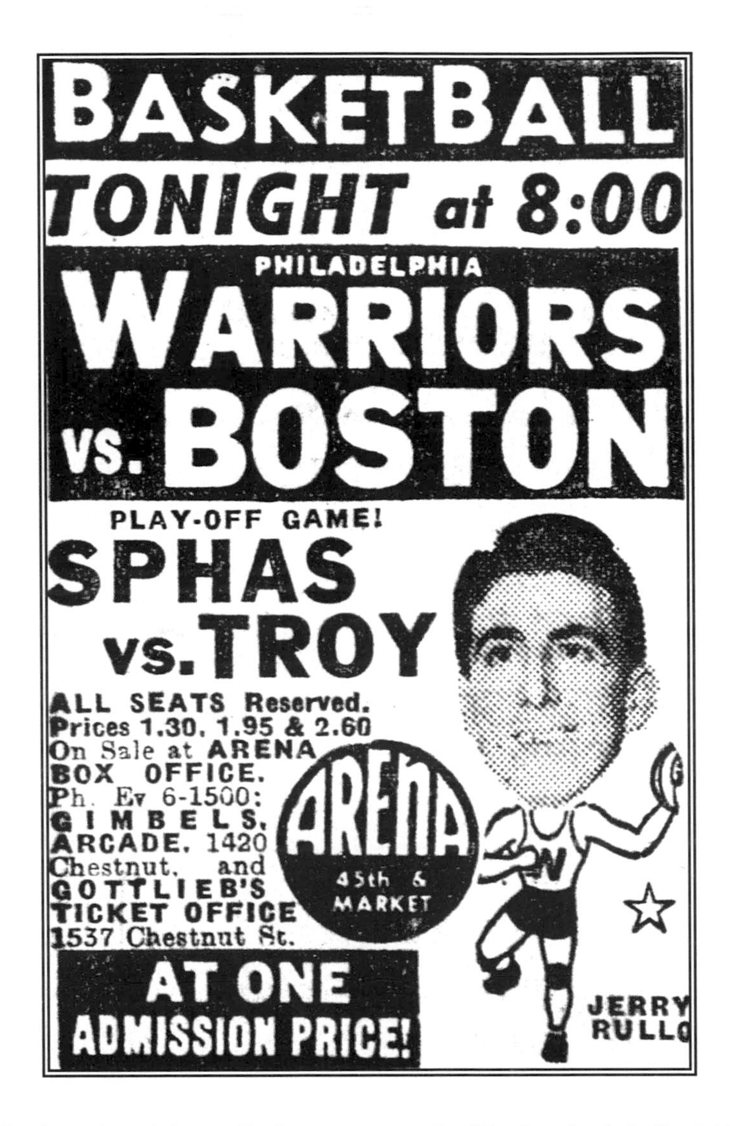

The SPHAS often played the preliminary game to the Warriors in their final ABL years, 1946-49.

Jerry Fleishman, SPHAS Guard, 1943-45. An All-American at NYU, he was drafted by Eddie Gottlieb as a sophomore in 1943. He was also drafted by the U.S. Military but managed to play for the SPHAS every weekend.

Eddie Lyons (SPHAS guard 1947-49) was a minor league pitcher with the Cincinnati Reds. He was even better on the hardwood and was picked by Eddie Gottlieb to play guard for the Warriors. But Lyons promised his family he would finish college at Temple, and refused to give up on his baseball career.

Bob Lojewski played for the SPHAS on their exhibition tours. Afterward, he received offers from the Warriors and the Rochester Royals, but went into private business. His son, Bob, later played for the St. Joseph's Hawks and was drafted by the Sacramento Kings.

THE PHILADELPHIA WARRIORS
1946-1962

After World War II, operators of the country's largest arenas realized that pro basketball could be a fine attraction to fill their arenas on dates not taken by pro hockey and college basketball games. In 1946, along with Walter Brown who owned the Boston Garden, Ned Irish who ran Madison Square Garden, and Maurice Podoloff whose family owned the arena in New Haven, Gottlieb formed the Basketball Association of America which developed into the NBA. Gottlieb founded and became coach and general manager of the Philadelphia Warriors. Seven years later he was able to buy the franchise for $25,000 and become the sole owner.

KLOTZ

> Abe Saperstein did a lot for the NBA in the early years and someone promised him the Laker franchise. Well, it turned out they gave it to someone else and Abe became so angry, he wanted nothing to do with the NBA. He sold his share of the Philadelphia Warriors to Eddie for $25,000 and that's how Eddie became sole owner of the team.

In 1946, the newly-formed Basketball Association of America consisted of 11 franchises including three which remain today: the Boston Celtics, the New York Knickerbockers, and the Philadelphia Warriors (now the Golden State Warriors).

The following year, four of the 11 franchises dropped out, and in 1948 were replaced by four teams from the National

Basketball League, a midwestern-based professional league that had existed since 1937. They were: the Ft. Wayne Pistons (now Detroit), the Minneapolis Lakers (now Los Angeles), the Rochester Royals (now the Sacramento Kings), and the Indianapolis Jets.

The Philadelphia Warriors played most of their home games at the Philadelphia Arena at 46th and Market to crowds as large as 8,500. When there were ice capades at the Arena, the team played at Convention Hall to a sometimes larger crowd of 12,000.

The roster was made up of ten players. The starting five were Angelo Musi from Temple, and George Senesky from St. Joe's at guards; Joe Fulks from Kentucky, and Howie Dallmar from Penn at forwards; and Art Hillhouse from LIU at center. A third guard in the rotation was Jerry Rullo from Temple who excelled on defense. Other players on the roster included guard Petey Rosenberg and Matt Guokas from St. Joe's, and Jerry Fleishman and Ralph Kaplowitz, both from NYU, who had played for the SPHAS. Guards Fred Sheffield from Utah, and John Murphy, a Philadelphian, began the season with the Warriors but left the team soon after.

JERRY RULLO
(GUARD, PHILADELPHIA
WARRIORS 1946-1947, 1948-50)

I always preferred playing at Convention Hall. The crowds were larger and the floor was better. At the Arena you had the ice floor underneath. And when

RULLO (Cont'd)
it was a warm day, the ice would sweat, seep through the floor and we'd slip all over the place and lose the ball.

ANGELO MUSI
(GUARD - PHILADELPHIA
WARRIORS 1946-49)
One night against Indianapolis the floor was so slippery we could hardly stand up. But Gotty had no intention of canceling the game, so on we went, and sometime we'd dribble the ball down court, hit a dead spot, and the ball wouldn't bounce back. Those times I wished the ice capades were there and we weren't.

In their first season in the newly-formed BAA, the Warriors met the Chicago Stags for the championship, and won the series behind the play of forward Joe Fulks, considered to be modern pro-basketball's first scoring sensation.

RULLO
Petey Rosenberg, one of our guards, had seen Joe play in the service and he told Gotty about him. That's how he came to us. He was a great player, a great guy and the fans loved him. He had the greatest variety of shots in the league. One- and two-handed set shots, a hook shot, and he was the first player in the League to use a jump shot. In his first year, he averaged over 23 points a game and led the league in scoring.

MUSI
In those days we had no 24 second clock and no 3 point play. So it was amazing to average the number of points that Joe did. The Knicks' coach Jack Lapchick used to say: "I give Fulks 25 points before the game starts."

RULLO

He made a lot of unbelievable baskets. Sometimes with two and three guys on him. And he was also a terrific rebounder off the defensive boards.

In his second year, Fulks won the scoring title again, averaging 22 points per game. In 1949 he scored a then NBA record of 63 points against Indianapolis. That same year the Sporting News called Fulks the greatest basketball player in the country.

PAUL ARIZIN
(FORWARD, PHILADELPHIA
WARRIORS 1950-52, 1954-62)

In my opinion, had it not been for Joe Fulks in the first two years of the League, the BAA would have folded. He was the biggest star, the biggest attraction and he carried the League. Soon after, George Mikan came in and helped Joe. But without those two, I don't think the League would have gotten past the early fifties.

MUSI

We all felt that over the years, Joe never got the recognition he deserved. He really helped to make the NBA outstanding. He was the Babe Ruth of basketball.

RULLO

Joe was a prolific scorer and a great showman. I can still remember the roar of the crowd when he put the ball in the basket. They got so enthused, they'd pick up the metal chairs they sat on and bang them on the floor. No one who saw him play will ever forget him.

In the early years of the League, Gottlieb proved to be a positive force. He always opposed anything that would deter excitement from the spectators. In the first year he was instrumental in outlawing the zone defense, because he and others felt it made the game more sluggish and slowed it down. Nearly every innovation or beneficial rule change in the NBA was either inspired by Gottlieb or influenced by his judgment. As chairman of the NBA Rules Committee for 25 years, Gottlieb was instrumental in the adoption of the 24-second rule, and the bonus penalty shot.

RULLO

> Gotty was a good coach and good for the League. It was his philosophy to recruit outstanding players who wanted to take the caliber of fast-paced inter-collegiate ball to a higher level. He was very high on players with skills and abilities to put the ball in the basket. And when we didn't put the ball in the basket, Eddie got very unhappy. He hated to lose. He would always give us our spending money and schedule before the game. Because if we lost, he took it hard and didn't want to talk to anybody.

MUSI

> I always enjoyed a good relationship with Gotty. But he could be a tough taskmaster who didn't mince words. After the first year I was the second leading scorer and captain of a championship team. So I went to Eddie and asked for a raise. When we sat down to negotiate he remembered every shot I missed and every bad pass I threw. I thought I was really in for it. Luckily, the general manager Pete Tyrell stepped in and agreed to split the difference.

GEORGE DEMPSEY
(GUARD, PHILADELPHIA
WARRIORS 1954-1958)

We were in New York playing the Knicks in the Garden and Joe Graboski was far ahead of everyone going in for a dunk. There were a lot of girls seated behind the basket and "Grabo" wanted to look good. He hit the back of the rim so hard, the ball bounced back to half court. Carl Braun grabbed it, scored, and we lost by 2 points. Well, we went into the locker room, and Gotty blew up. He said he was learning new ways to lose from his ball club, so he invented some curse words I never heard before. And when he got angry, it was best to look at the floor. Because if you looked at him, you would get it worse than the guy who did it.

The overall style of the game remained unchanged in the 1940s and in the new NBA. Fundamental basketball was still the top priority.

MUSI

We played team ball. We'd pass and work for the shot. Dribbling was not a common thing. Gotty would say: "Dribble after you fake your man on the way to the basket. Or if you take it off the board and can't pass it out and get free." We relied a lot on passing and quite often we'd pass between us until we got to mid-court.

RULLO

We always played good defense. You stayed with your man through hell and high water. And I always took pride in playing defense because we all felt it was a very important part of the game.

MUSI

The nice thing about our group was the attitude of the players. We all liked each other and enjoyed playing together. There was a closeness. That doesn't exist today.

RULLO

If I was upstairs getting dressed, Angelo, Howie and Joe would wait for me and then we'd all go out to dinner together. Not like today where everybody does their own thing. We didn't make a lot of money, but we loved playin' ball and were happy.

Gottlieb never had an off-season. He was always involved in some phase of basketball. He never took a wife because he was already married — to the game of basketball. He served as NBA's solo schedule-maker for almost 20 years. He also organized overseas tours of the Harlem Globetrotters, promoted NBA doubleheaders, and pro wrestling as well.

CAMPBELL

The mogul had an amazing mind when it came to numbers and figures. I would ask him at an away game how big he thought the house was. He'd glance up in the stands, turn to me and say, "12,000." And the official attendance would be 12,150.

In 1949, the six remaining teams from the National Basketball League joined the Basketball Association of America and it became the 17 member National Basketball Association. New or recent arrivals to the team were guards Chink Crossin from Penn and Nelson Bobb from Temple, Gale Bishop, a scorer from out west, and center Ed Sadowski from Seton Hall. By the 1950-51 season, the League was down to 10 teams.

Joining the roster that season was consensus All-American Paul Arizin from Villanova. Without any high school experience, Arizin made the Villanova team as a sophomore with hard work and perseverance. A year later he set a single game record by scoring 85 points, and as a senior, led the nation in scoring with 25.3 points per game. With a textbook perfect jump shot, Arizin was the first round choice of the Philadelphia Warriors.

WASHINGTON

> I can remember playing against Paul in an independent league in the PTC building at 20th and Johnson. Someone told me he had asthma. He sure didn't have it on the basketball court. He ran everybody off the floor. In my opinion, he was one of the best players ever to come out of Philadelphia.

ARIZIN

> In my rookie year, I was fortunate to join a team that had three outstanding players: George Senesky and Andy Phillip at guards, and Joe Fulks at forward. George Senesky was an excellent player and a very tough guard who had played on the championship team. Andy Phillip was a great player, a great passer, probably one of the best passers I ever played with, and Joe Fulks was already an established star.

In 1950 the new NBA was just beginning to grow. There was a question as to whether it would continue. In an effort to attract the fans, most of the NBA games were doubleheaders. So

Gottlieb put his friendship and partnership with Abe Saperstein, owner of the Harlem Globetrotters, to good use.

HARVEY POLLACK
(PUBLIC RELATIONS DIRECTOR - STATISTICIAN, PHILADELPHIA WARRIORS - 1946-62)

He made a deal with Saperstein that wherever the Globetrotters played, he would bring an NBA home game to that site. So the Warriors played home games all over the country, in towns like Saratoga Springs, NY, Toledo, Ohio, and New Haven, Conn. And I had to travel with the team because the rules stated the home team had to provide the scorekeeper and statistician. So we played the first game of a doubleheader but at that time, the Globetrotters were the big attraction, not the NBA.

WASHINGTON

When the NBA began playing doubleheaders with the Harlem Globetrotters to attract attention, we would play first and the NBA teams would go second. But after the Globetrotters finished playing, everybody went home and the NBA teams played to an empty house. So the League decided to make the NBA the preliminary game. That way, they had an audience who were waiting to see us.

DEMPSEY

One night we were playing the St. Louis Hawks in Albany. It was a long day and that night I played almost the whole game. At the very end I got fouled going in and I was so tired I asked Jack George if he would shoot for me. After the game the ref said, "Hey, Dempsey, did you shoot those two foul shots?" I said, "No. I was too tired. Jack shot 'em." "That's not allowed," he said. "Okay,"

DEMPSEY (Cont'd)
I said. He couldn't do anything. The game was over. That season, Jack George had a thousand points. Two of those were mine. The next season, the head of officials came to our camp with the new rule changes. And he said with great emphasis: "Whenever you get fouled, you shoot your own foul shots."

In 1950, the Warriors won the Eastern Division title with Fulks hitting his stroke at 18.7 points per game, and solid contributions from Arizin and Andy Phillip who led the League in assists. But Philadelphia was stunned by the Syracuse Nationals who swept the first two games of the best-of-three series.

The following year Paul Arizin paced the Warriors with over 25 points per game, surpassing George Mikan to win the League's scoring title. 1952 was also the first year of the expanded 12 foot foul line, a rule aimed at limiting Mikan's dominance. Arizin joined the Marines for two years and Joe Fulks retired before his return. So three seasons, from 1952-55, were down years for the club, finishing fourth and fifth in the Eastern Division.

The one bright spot was Neil Johnston who had joined the team in 1950 after a relatively obscure college career at Ohio State.

ARIZIN
I think in college Neil enjoyed the baseball diamond more than the hardwood. In fact, he was a minor league pitcher with the Phillies when a sore arm and bad luck ended his career. But their loss was our gain.

Gottlieb saw Johnston's potential and signed the 6 foot 8 big man as a free agent. He became a multi-dimensional player with a devastating, sweeping hook shot from the pivot. From 1952 to 1955 he led the League in scoring and in rebounding one year as well. Through eight NBA seasons, he averaged almost 20 points and 11 rebounds per game.

By 1954, the NBA was down to eight teams. The Eastern Conference consisted of the New York Knicks, the Boston Celtics, the Syracuse Nationals, and the Philadelphia Warriors. In the west: the Minneapolis Lakers, Ft. Wayne Pistons, Milwaukee Hawks, and Rochester Royals.

By the mid-1950s the teams played about 72 games a season and the play-off schedule worked like this: the second and third place teams in each division would play each other in a 3 or 5 game series; the winner would play the first place team, and then the two division winners would meet for the championship. 1954 was also the first year the League inserted the 24-second clock and the bonus free throw for team fouls. This made the game a little quicker and less foul prone.

ARIZIN

> Prior to the 24-second rule, it was not uncommon toward the end of a game for a team that was leading to hold the ball and not attempt to shoot it. This wasn't very attractive to the fans. In fact, one thing that burns in my memory occurred my first year. We won the Eastern Division and played Syracuse in the play-offs. The first game at the Arena went into overtime. We got the center jump,

ARIZIN (Cont'd)
missed the shot, they got the rebound, held the ball for four minutes and 50 seconds, took the last shot and beat us. And that eliminated us from the play-offs.

POLLACK
Danny Biasone, the owner of the Syracuse Nationals came up with the formula for the 24-second rule: each team averaged about 60 shots a game. Multiply that by two teams and it gives you 120 shots. Divide that into 2880 seconds in a 48-minute game and it comes out to exactly 24 seconds.

In 1955, the Warriors featured a slightly revamped team to complement Arizin and Johnston. Tom Gola, a Philadelphia folk hero from LaSalle, was a four-time All American and Player of the Year. He averaged almost 21 points and 19 rebounds per game, had quick hands, deceptive speed and was a complete player. He was just the spark the Warriors needed.

The remainder of the team included guard Jack George, also from LaSalle, Joe Graboski, a big, strong forward with an outside shot, from the Indianapolis Jets, who never played college ball, veteran guard George Dempsey from Kings College who had played with the SPHAS, Ernie Beck, a guard-forward from Penn who rejoined the Warriors after completing his tour of military service, forward Jackie Moore from LaSalle, back-up guard Larry Hennessey from Villanova, and Walter Davis, a high-jump champion from Texas A&M, who was the back-up center.

Shortly before the season began, Gottlieb resigned as coach due to health reasons, and turned the duties over to former Warriors guard, George Senesky.

ARIZIN

> I think George was a very fine coach. He had played the game, understood it, and really understood the mentality of the player. He spoke in plain terms, communicated well and to this day I don't understand why he was replaced.

That season, the Warriors won the Eastern Division with a record of 45-27. They beat the Syracuse Nationals in a tough 5-game series, then defeated the Ft. Wayne Pistons in the finals to win their second championship.

ARIZIN

> What I find different about the game today is a lot of what you see are guys getting open on switching defenses, and taking an open jump shot. In my day, you had to work more to get open and get your shot. When you did, there was more driving to the basket and more lay-ups made. There's too much emphasis on the 3-point shot — a lot of players depend on it and when they're not hitting, they have a bad night. We would score much closer to the basket to compensate. On defense, the theory in my day was that's your man. If you can't stop him, we'll get somebody in there that can. It seems today, if you let your man go past you and he scores, it's not your fault. It's the man behind you who didn't pick him up. Yeh, we switched in our day, but not unless you had to. It happens more often today because everybody tries to gang up, double team and steal the ball. I think individual defense was better in my day. Today, emphasis is more on team defense, which is what the zone defense really is.

GOLA
(GUARD, PHILADELPHIA
WARRIORS 1955-56, 1957-62)

I think today's game is unbalanced. A lot of teams have one or sometimes two players that carry the load. I don't believe in all that concentration offensively with one player. You have to have more than that. If he has a good night, you might win a lot. But if not, you have a problem. Another concern is a lot of things don't get called today. But I understand why. It would be bad for TV and bad for attendance. That's what the game is predicated on, and that's where the money is. So there are things the League condones and the referee allows. It was the same when I played. There were all-stars who took a step before their jump shot. Another player had a behind-the-back dribble — that's walking. But they never called it because it would have put them out of the game.

WASHINGTON

The kids today are big, talented and very athletic. They do stuff we didn't do. But they don't play smart and they don't learn basic basketball skills. Lots of these kids come off the playground and don't want to listen. They think they know it all. If they get to the pros, they wind up playin' for stats and money, and they don't play defense. In the low post they try to lean on the man and get physical instead of frontin' him and denyin' him the ball. Zach Clayton used to say: "When is a man dangerous? When he has the ball. He can't hurt you if he don't have the ball." So your position is to deny him the pass. I used to circle my man. I'd be in front of him when he was back, I'd be behind him when he was way out. He didn't know where I was. Today these guys are leaning, pushing, shoving, and that's no good because then your man

WASHINGTON (Cont'd)
knows where you are. A center man shouldn't know where you are when you're playing defense. I like a player who plays smart. A guy who looks for his open teammate, passes the ball, takes his shot when he has it, and plays defense. Makes the players around him better by the way he plays the game.

KLOTZ
Because these kids are growin' so big, eventually they're going to have to raise the basket. When the game originated over 100 years ago, the average player was 5'5". Today he's almost a foot taller. Now they have centers coming into the league that are 7 ½ feet tall. It won't be long before a player stands underneath with an extended hand way beyond the basket and dumps everything in. Raising the basket may cut down on 3-point shooting, but they complain about that anyway.

After the Warriors won their second championship, Red Auerbach, Boston Celtic coach, made a series of moves that would impact the NBA for the next thirteen years. Auerbach took Holy Cross sensation Tom Heinsohn, then traded center Ed Macauley and draftee Cliff Hagan to the St. Louis Hawks for the rights to Bill Russell, who had led the University of San Francisco to an NCAA title. With an explosive back court of Bob Cousy and Bill Sharman, and forward Frank Ramsey returning from the service, the pieces were in place for Boston to win. Russell was everything Auerbach had hoped for and more. He was ferocious on the boards, and intimidating on defense. And when he stepped onto the court, he gave the Celtics a new personality.

DEMPSEY

> Russell took great pride in playing defense. And he did everything he could to help his team win the game. He'd rebound, pass; even when he blocked a shot, he'd try to keep the ball in bounds so one of his teammates could get it.

In the fall of 1957, Lenny Rosenbluth, a shooter from North Carolina, and Woody Sauldsberry, a former Globetrotter with a great outside shot, joined the Warriors and Woody was Rookie of the Year. But the years 1956-59 proved difficult. Tom Gola was inducted into the service, and injuries to Arizin and Johnston hampered the team. The Warriors finished 37-35 two years in a row and lost to Boston in the play-offs.

The following year, George Senesky was replaced by Al Cervi, and three new players joined the team. Guy Rodgers, a guard from Temple University, former Harlem Globetrotter Andy Johnson from Portland, and Vern Hatton from Kentucky came aboard for the 1958-59 season.

SHRIER

> Everyone always thought of Guy Rodgers as a playmaker and passer, but what a lot of people don't know is that Guy was the highest scorer in the history of Temple basketball with 1760 points for many years. But he was a master with the ball. He had tremendous speed, always had control, and he never minded giving up the ball because he had great delight in handing out assists.

WASHINGTON

Guy was a wonderful ball player without equal. One of the fastest guards I ever saw, a terrific ball handler and a great passer. He could do everything off the run and always find the open man, not like these guys today that give the ball up in self-defense. I don't think he has an equal in the NBA today.

ERNIE BECK
(GUARD, PHILADELPHIA
WARRIORS 1953-60)

Andy Johnson was a very good defender and although he was only about 6'5", he helped us a lot in the low post. He was very strong and tough. He was the kind of guy you didn't want to mess with. One night here against New York, Richie Guerin and Guy Sparrow got into a fight with Andy and Woody, and before you knew it, we were all involved. It spilled onto the front row, benches tumbled and just then I remembered my father was there, seated in the front row. So I looked over to see if he was all right and he had Guy Sparrow in a headlock.

GERSH

I remember taking my father to that game, which was his first, and watching that brawl. And I'll never forget coming out of Convention Hall and him saying, "Simcha, if that's basketball, I think I like it!"

ARIZIN

Al Cervi, our new coach, had played with the Rochester Royals and Syracuse Nationals, and coached them in the 1950s. He was a tough competitor and a self-made man. But he and Gotty were not a good match. They were both very strong individuals, and Al didn't like to take Gotty's suggestions. He chose to run things his own way

ARIZIN (Cont'd)

and Gotty didn't like that. Al also never moved to Philadelphia. He commuted from New York, and that was an awkward set-up. In his defense, Neil Johnston re-injured his leg and was out most of the season. So we played almost the whole year without a center, finished 32-40 and out of the play-offs.

BECK

Al Cervi was a very competitive guy by nature and although he was no longer playing in the NBA, he still loved to challenge his players to a game. So quite often at practice, while most of us would shoot around at one end, Al would be playing one-on-one with Jack George or somebody else at the other basket. Well, one day we're out in St. Louis having a practice, and Al is playing at the far end and either gets knocked down or collapses from exhaustion. Just then a reporter comes in to interview the coach and asks Tommy Gola where he is. So we point to the other end and the reporter says, "Which one?" And we said, "The guy lying flat on his rear end."

The following year Cervi was fired. Center Neil Johnston retired and became head coach of the Warriors for the 1959-60 season.

As the NBA grew and teams tried to build a local fan base, the draft included territorial picks. A team was permitted to select a player who played his college ball in the immediate area of the franchise before the regular draft, and forfeit its first-round pick.

Ironically, Eddie Gottlieb had planted the seed four years earlier.

POLLACK

In 1955, Gotty realized how great Wilt was by watching him at Overbrook High School. So he had an NBA rule passed where he could pick his No. 1 draft choice for four years later (when Wilt was eligible). Two weeks later, the other NBA owners realized they had been rope-a-doped, and had the rule rescinded. But Wilt was already on the books as the Warriors' number one draft pick in 1959.

Wilt Chamberlain was the League's scoring and rebounding leader and an all-star in his rookie season. His numbers were astounding - 37.6 points and 27 rebounds per game, and at season's end, he was named the League's Most Valuable Player, and Player of the Year.

Teamed with Paul Arizin, Tom Gola, Guy Rodgers and Woody Sauldsberry, Chamberlain paced Philadelphia to a 49-26 record, finishing second behind Boston in the Eastern Division. The Warriors defeated Syracuse in the play-offs to meet the Celtics in the Eastern Division finals. The series was tied 1-1 when Chamberlain got into a fight with Celtic forward Tommy Heinsohn and broke his hand.

ARIZIN

On the foul line, when we shot, Wilt would have the inside position. Heinsohn would be next to him and when the shot went up, Heinsohn would step in front of Wilt to prevent him from running down court and Russell would fast break. They did that a lot to him and finally Wilt had enough.

GOLA

> I had my hand on Heinsohn's chest, trying to push him away, and I caught one of Wilt's punches. My arm swelled up to the size of a golf ball, and I thought it was broken. Fortunately, it wasn't, and that was the last time I tried to play peacemaker.

With Wilt handicapped, the Celtics won the next two and were ready to celebrate when the Warriors beat them badly in the fifth game at Boston Garden. It was now 3-2 with the sixth game in Philly. With seconds to go and the score tied, Bill Sharman missed a shot. Heinsohn tapped it in and Philadelphia was out of the play-offs. But many felt the Warriors would have won the series had Wilt not broken his hand.

ARIZIN

> Wilt was known for his great strength, but he also had an incredible ability to withstand pain. One afternoon we were playing the Hawks in St. Louis, and Clyde Lovelette was their center. Clyde could be mean-spirited and you didn't want to get behind his elbows. Unfortunately, Wilt did and went down. We went over and it looked like he had gotten his teeth knocked out. So we began to look for them on the floor. What had happened was when he caught the elbow, it pushed the teeth up into his jawbone.

GOLA

> When he came into the dressing room, I didn't recognize him. His face had swelled up, his eyes were closed, his sinuses were infected, he looked like a different person. That was really a shame.

ARIZIN

We went to New York the next day to play the Knicks. Wilt went to a dentist, and was back in the line-up a few days later. He missed one game.

Al Attles from North Carolina A&T joined the back court the following year. Gone were veteran guards Ernie Beck to the Hawks, Jack George to the Knicks, and George Dempsey to Syracuse. Other new arrivals included Ed Conlan, Joe Ruklick and Bill "Pickles" Kennedy. The 1960-61 season was more of the same, particularly more of Wilt Chamberlain. Once again, he led the League in scoring with 38.4 points per game, and hauled in a League high 27.2 rebounds per game. But despite his brilliance, and a 46-33 record, the Celtics had the better team, finishing 11 games ahead of Philadelphia in the Eastern Division. In the 1961 NBA play-offs, Philadelphia was surprisingly swept by Syracuse in the semifinals and Boston again won the title.

ARIZIN

Boston had Cousy, Sharman, Russell, Heinsohn, Ramsey, K.C. and Sam Jones. That's seven players I played against and they're all in the Hall of Fame. And Auerbach had a great ability to bring all of them together to play as a team.

GOLA

Auerbach had great talent he could bring in off the bench. Behind Cousy and Sharman, he had K.C. Jones and Sam Jones. When Frank Ramsey got old, he replaced him with John Havlicek. Beside Russell and Heinsohn, he had Jungle Jim Loscutoff and Satch Sanders. Most teams had five or six

GOLA (Cont'd)

guys, but he was loaded on the bench. And he could spell anybody.

For the 1961-62 season, the team drafted Tom Meschery from St. Mary's College in California and Ted Luckenbill from Houston to replace Woody Sauldsberry who was traded to the St. Louis Hawks the year before, and Andy Johnson who signed with Chicago. Head coach Neil Johnston was replaced by Frank McGuire from North Carolina.

GOLA

Wilt and Neil never saw eye-to-eye. Wilt brought certain offensive tools with him. He had the finger-roll lay-up, and the fade-away jumper he liked to use. Neil was more interested in having him play the pivot the way he did, and take that little hook shot. But Wilt didn't want to hear that. He was interested in being perceived as a versatile ball player and that's where the conflict came in.

Chamberlain made the 1961-62 season memorable. He averaged an NBA record 50.4 points per game, snagging 25.7 rebounds per contest. Some nights were mind-boggling. In a three-overtime gut-wrenching game against the Lakers on December 8, Chamberlain poured in 78 points. He scored 73 points against Chicago on January 13, and recorded three 62-point games in an eight game stretch, then came the unthinkable. On March 2, 1962, against New York in Hershey, PA, Chamberlain registered the League's only 100-point game.

POLLACK

Wilt was 36 for 63 from the field, and 28 of 32 from the foul line. In fact, that season he registered more points — 4029 — than minutes — 3886. That night, March 2, 1962 was by far the busiest night in my 56 year career. I was the public relations director for the Warriors and their game statistician. This game didn't mean anything because it was late in the season and neither team could move up in the standings. So the Inquirer asked me to cover it because they didn't want to send a writer. I was already the stringer for UPI and the AP man didn't know anything about basketball so I covered it for them as well. By the second half everyone heard on Bill Campbell's radio broadcast, about the way Wilt was scoring, and all of a sudden there were tons of reporters and photographers from all over covering the game. When it ended, I went to the dressing room because I knew they would want something for Wilt to take his picture with. Someone suggested the ball, but that was being autographed around the room. So I grabbed a piece of paper, scribbled a "100" on it and handed it to Wilt just as his picture was taken. In fact, my wife said she never saw me write so clearly.

Finishing second to Boston with a 49-31 record, the Warriors beat the Syracuse Nationals in the Eastern Division semi-finals. In the finals against Boston, tied at three games apiece going into the seventh game, Philadelphia lost by two points on a controversial goal-tending call. Again, Boston defeated the Western Conference team and won the championship.

ARIZIN

Russell was a great player, and his record of winning 11 championships in 13 years is amazing.

ARIZIN (Cont'd)

But Wilt did more than hold his own against him. A lot of people have the incorrect opinion that because Russell's team won the majority of games, he was better than Wilt and out-played him. That's not true. The real truth is that Boston had a better team than Philly. And that's why they beat us.

GOLA

On offense there was no comparison. Wilt was an offensive player without equal. And when he would concentrate on defense, nobody compared to him either. Bob Cousy made an interesting point once. He said when Russell came to the game you knew what you were getting. He would play defense and get rebounds. You never knew what you were going to get from Wilt. Sometimes he would go for the points, or the rebounds, or assists. But I always felt when Wilt concentrated on something, he could do anything he wanted. And I always said if I were choosing a team he would be my number one pick.

ARIZIN

You have to understand something about Wilt. He never wanted to be accepted as a great basketball player because he was big. That was very onerous to him. He hated the term "Wilt the Stilt." He wanted to be accepted as a complete basketball player. Not as someone that accomplished things because he was 7'1". So he went through phases where he wanted to show how good he could score or rebound or pass the ball. I believe he is the only center or one of the only centers to ever hold the NBA record for assists in a season. Wilt was a complex player, but certainly a great one.

AL ATTLES
(GUARD, PHILADELPHIA
WARRIORS 1960-62)

The minute you start to compare Bill Russell to Wilt because of all the championships he won, you take it out of individual context, and you can't do that. It's a team game and no one individual wins a team sport. Russell enabled them to win as a team. And when all is said and done, the Celtics were a better team. That's the way it was and there's no sense in diluting that.

POLLACK

A lot of people attribute Wilt's feats to his size. But he was a true, natural athlete, with exceptional speed, agility and strength. He was the greatest player I ever saw, and I've seen them all.

ATTLES

I wish people could have known him in other respects. He was a much deeper, caring person than people gave him credit for. He was a very special man, both on and off the court.

ARIZIN

When I was playing my last year with the Warriors, my son Michael would come to a few games with me and Wilt got to know him. When Michael grew up and married, he had a son and a daughter, and at age 15, his daughter Stephanie was stricken with an inoperable brain tumor. Somehow Wilt found out about it, not through me, and he corresponded with her. He wrote her several letters and this cheered her up immeasurably. In 1997 when Wilt and I were selected to the 50 Greatest NBA Players, the ceremony was held in Cleveland at the All-Star game. Stephanie begged her father to take her. She was in very bad shape then. He agreed and who

ARIZIN (Cont'd)

> came over and greeted Stephanie but Wilt. He pushed her around in her wheelchair the whole evening. One thing she wanted was to get all the autographs of the players. That was difficult because some players don't like to give them. But Wilt made sure he got every autograph for her. That shows what kind of person he was. And he kept up contact with Stephanie until her death a few months later. It takes a special man to do that.

The Philadelphia Warriors moved to San Francisco after the 1961-62 season. Eddie Gottlieb sold the franchise for $850,000 to a credit card company, and later a consortium of owners was formed. He stayed with the team for two years as the General Manager, then moved back to Philadelphia.

Not content to retire, Gottlieb continued to work as a consultant to the NBA. By 1968, he was making an 82-game schedule for 14 teams in two divisions that had 14 different ideas how their schedule should be. He did it without a computer, on yellow-lined paper, made revisions on cocktail napkins, and was able to fulfill everyone's wishes. Said head coach Bill Fitch, "He's the one guy who told me where to go and then I couldn't wait to get there."

Never accused of being a pacifist when he coached, Gottlieb was charitable and good-hearted. When Harry Litwack needed money to open his basketball camp, Gottlieb loaned him $50,000. He also put together a display for the Hall of Fame as a salute to the men who played for him. It took him a whole year and cost him $10,000.

In the mid to late 70s, Gottlieb was able to see Tom Gola, Paul Arizin, Joe Fulks, and Wilt Chamberlain inducted into the Naismith Memorial Basketball Hall of Fame.

Then on December 7, 1979 Eddie Gottlieb, from South Philadelphia by way of the Ukraine, passed away at the age of 81. The Chapel on North Broad Street was packed with basketball dignitaries who came from all over to say good-bye. Gottlieb would have appreciated that. He always liked to play to a full house.

The Philadelphia SPHAS are prominently honored in the Naismith Memorial Basketball Hall of Fame in Springfield, Massachusetts; and at the International Jewish Sports Hall of Fame at Wingate Institute in Israel.

The San Francisco Warriors began play in the 1963-64 season. In 1971, the team moved across the bay to Oakland, became the Golden State Warriors and remain so today.

Each season, the NBA Rookie of the year is awarded the Eddie Gottlieb Trophy.

1956 World Champion Philadelphia Warriors warm-up jacket.
(NBA Hardwood Classics)
Offered by Mitchell and Ness Nostalgia Co., 1229 Walnut Sreet, Philadelphia, PA 19107

WARRIORS

1946–1962

Joe Fulks was the first superstar in the NBA. He played 8 years with the Warriors, then retired in 1954. (Philadelphia Inquirer)

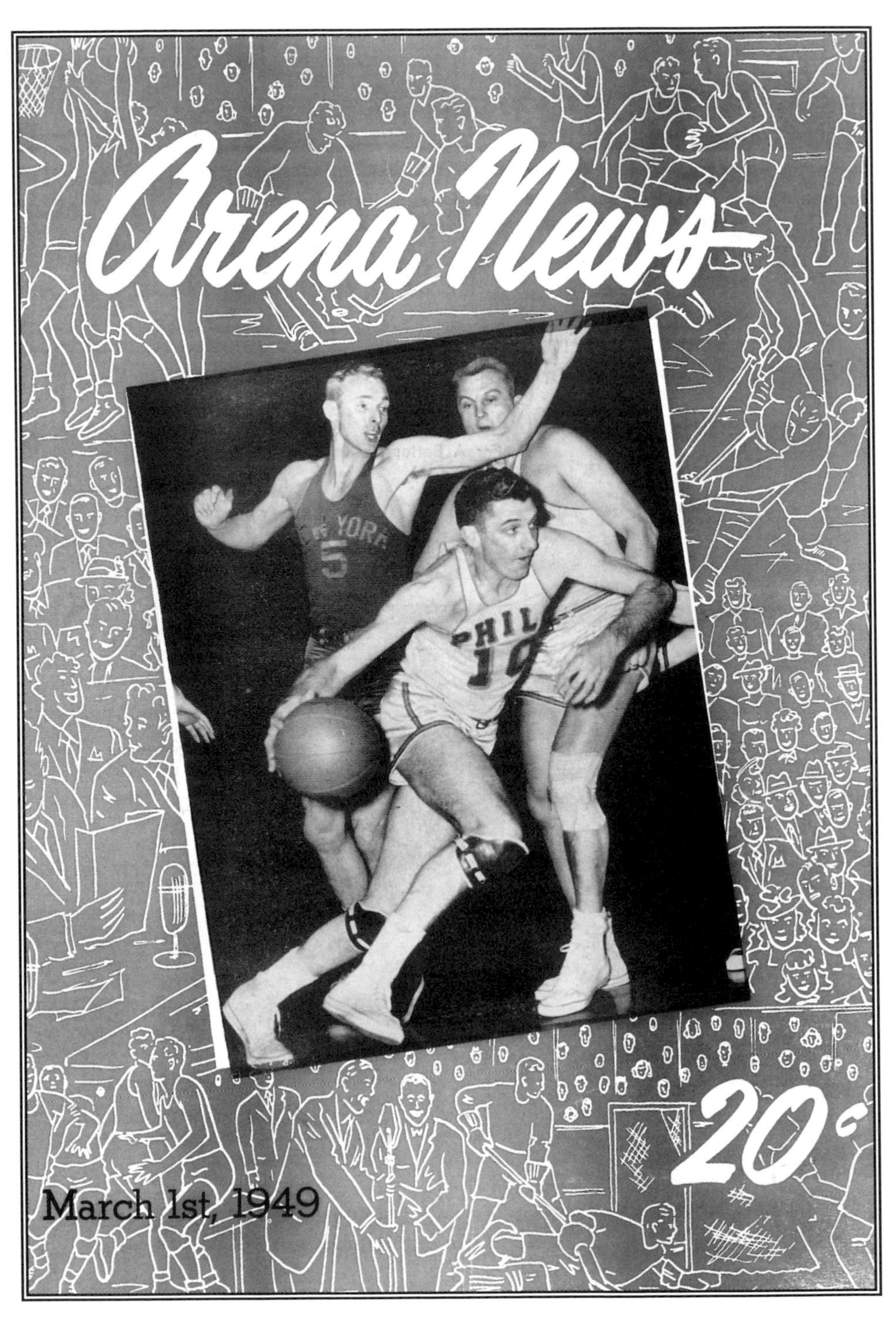

Joe Lapchick, the Knicks coach, would say: "I give Joe Fulks 25 points before the game starts."

1947 program. A few months later these two teams would meet for the BAA Championship.

1946-47 Warriors team. Top row: Fred Sheffield, Matt Guokas, Joe Fulks, Art Hillhouse, Howie Dallmar, George Senesky. Bottom row: Angelo Musi, Jerry Rullo, John Murphy, Jerry Fleishman, Petey Rosenberg.

Jerry Rullo, a guard from Temple University, was an exceptional defensive player with the Warriors in the late 1940s.

Angelo Musi teamed with George Senesky in the back court for three years (1946-49).

Jerry Fleishman - as a Philadelphia Warrior 1946-50, 1952-53.

1948-49 Philadelphia Warriors. Top row, L to R: Gale Bishop, Howie Dallmar, Jake Bornheimer, Ed Sadowski, Joe Fulks, Irv Torgoff. Bottom row, seated, L to R: Pete Tyrell, Jerry Fleishman, Chink Crossin, Angelo Musi, George Senesky, Jerry Rullo, Eddie Gottlieb. (Philadelphia Daily News)

Forward Howie Dallmar blocks a shot in a 1948 game vs. the Rochester Royals. Each Warrior took pride in his defense. (Temple University Urban Archives)

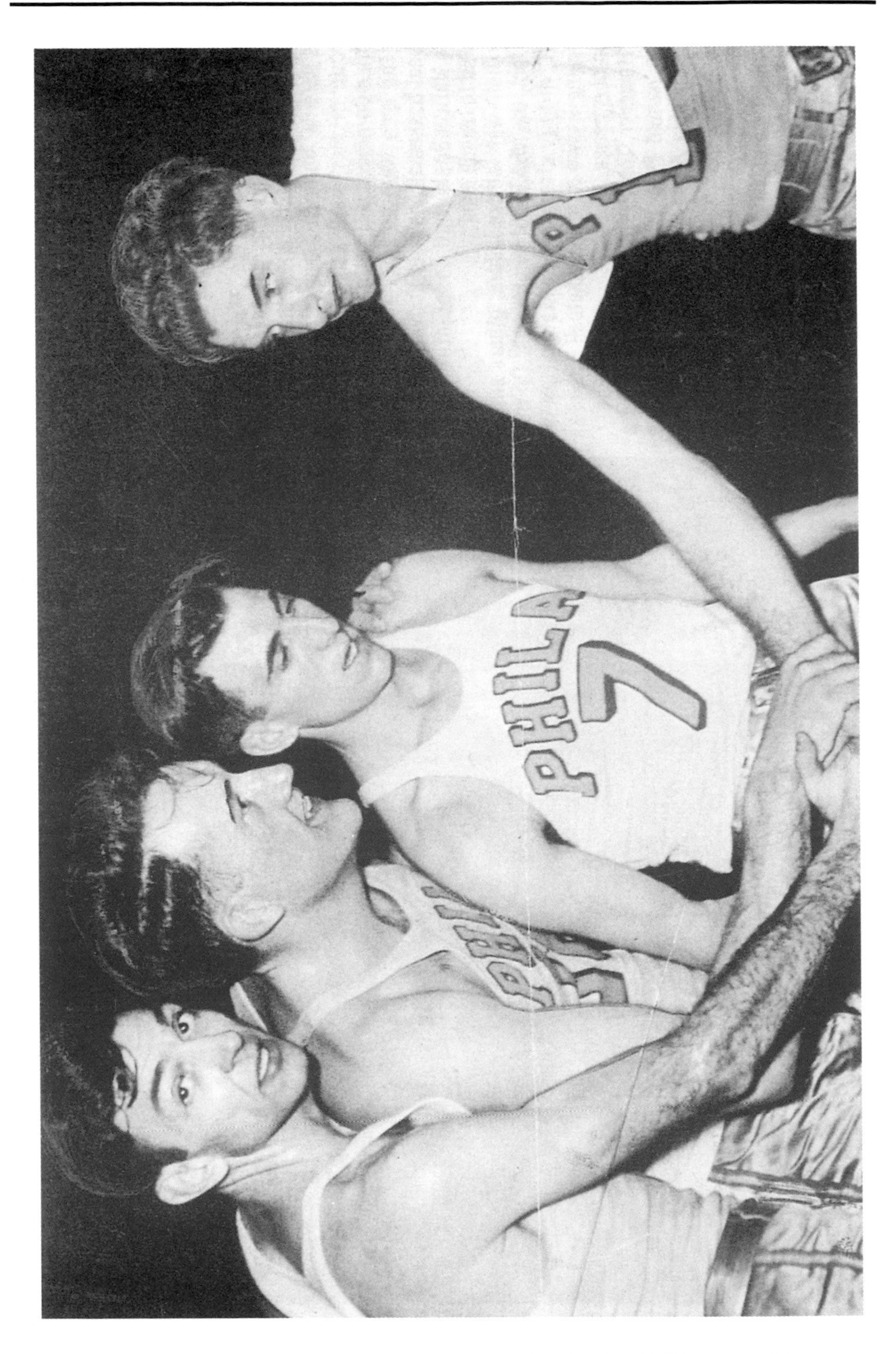

Joe Fulks is congratulated by teammates Ralph Kaplowitz, Art Hillhouse and Jerry Rullo on scoring 1000 points.

Paul Arizin, with a textbook perfect jump shot, joined the Warriors in 1950, and became one of the top players in NBA history. (Temple University Urban Archives)

In 1952 Paul Arizin joined the Marines, and Joe Fulks retired before his return in 1954. That spelled trouble for the Warriors. (Philadelphia Inquirer)

Eddie Gottlieb ponders the future in his "crystal basketball." (Temple University Urban Archives)

Neil Johnston was a bright spot from 1952-55. (Temple University Urban Archives)

With a devastating, sweeping hook shot from the pivot, Johnston led the league in scoring three years in a row. (Temple University Urban Archives)

In an effort to draw and build a fan base, many NBA doubleheaders were played in the 1950s.

George Dempsey, a high scorer from Kings College, played good defense for the Warriors from 1954-58.

Ernie Beck, from Penn, was a Warrior guard from 1953-60.

Tom Gola was a Philadelphia folk hero and a four-time All-American from LaSalle. (Temple University Urban Archives)

Gola was just the spark the Warriors needed. (Temple University Urban Archives)

Gola scores over Celtic guard Bill Sharman while Bob Cousy watches, in March 1960. (Temple University Urban Archives)

Jack George (a gifted athlete from LaSalle and Notre Dame), Joe Graboski (who never played college ball) and Tom Gola, pictured in September of 1958. (Temple University Urban Archives)

Jack George is undeterred by Jim Loscutoff of the Celtics on November 11, 1955. (Temple University Urban Archives)

Paul Arizin on his way to the promised land, January 14, 1955. (Temple University Urban Archives)

The 1956 Championship team.

Harvey Pollack smokes his first cigar (with Neil Johnston and Paul Arizin) to celebrate the 1956 Championship.

Eddie Gottlieb was a founder, owner, coach, player, administrator and promoter. He was a canny businessman, colorful personality and knew the game of basketball inside and out. He loved to win and hated to lose. (Temple University Urban Archives)

Bill Russell was ferocious on the boards and intimidating on defense. He made the Celtics a different team. (Temple University Urban Archives)

Woody Sauldsberry: Rookie of the Year 1957-58. (Temple University Urban Archives)

Guy Rodgers was the definitive point guard and some say without equal today. (Temple University Urban Archives)

Harry Litwack and Guy Rodgers in 1958. Litwack played six seasons with the SPHAS, 1930-36, coached them from 1946-49, was an assistant coach with the Philadelphia Warriors from 1949-51, and then became head coach at Temple University for 21 years. (Temple University Urban Archives)

1958-59 Philadelphia Warriors

Top Row L to R: Lenny Rosenbluth, Andy Johnson, Woody Sauldsberry, Neil Johnston, Joe Graboski, Tom Gola. Seated L to R: Phil Rollins, Jack George, Ernie Beck, Coach Al Cervi, Paul Arizin, George Dempsey, Guy Rodgers.

Eddie Gottlieb hires Neil Johnston in 1959 as head coach of the Warriors. Johnston was replaced in 1961 by Frank McGuire. (Temple University Urban Archives)

Norman Wilton Chamberlain, selected by the Philadelphia Warriors as a future draft pick in 1955, joined the team in 1959. (Temple University Urban Archives)

The 1959-1960 team.

Standing L to R: Eddie Gottlieb, Andy Johnson, Joe Ruklick, Wilt Chamberlain, Joe Graboski, Woody Sauldsberry, Neil Johnston. Seated L to R: Tom Gola, Ernie Beck, Paul Arizin, Guy Rodgers, Vern Hatton.

Wilt vs. Cincinnati Royals on December 10, 1959. He averaged 37.6 points per game his rookie year. (Temple University Urban Archives)

Wilt vs. The Minneapolis Lakers on November 11, 1959. He hauled in 27 rebounds per game. (Temple University Urban Archives)

Wilt's blocks were never recorded officially. Said Harvey Pollack, "If they were, he would have averaged in double figures." (Temple University Urban Archives)

The fight between Wilt and Tom Heinsohn in the third Warrior-Celtic play-off game in 1960. Wilt broke his hand and the Celtics won the series.

1960-61
PHILADELPHIA
Warriors
EDDIE
GOTTLIEB
WILT CHAMBERLAIN
NEIL JOHNSTON
PAUL ARIZIN
TOM GOLA
GUY
RODGERS
BILL KENNEDY
AL
ATTLES
ANDY
JOHNSON
JOE GRABOSKI
ED CONLIN
JOE
RUKLICK
VERN
HATTON

1960-61 team.

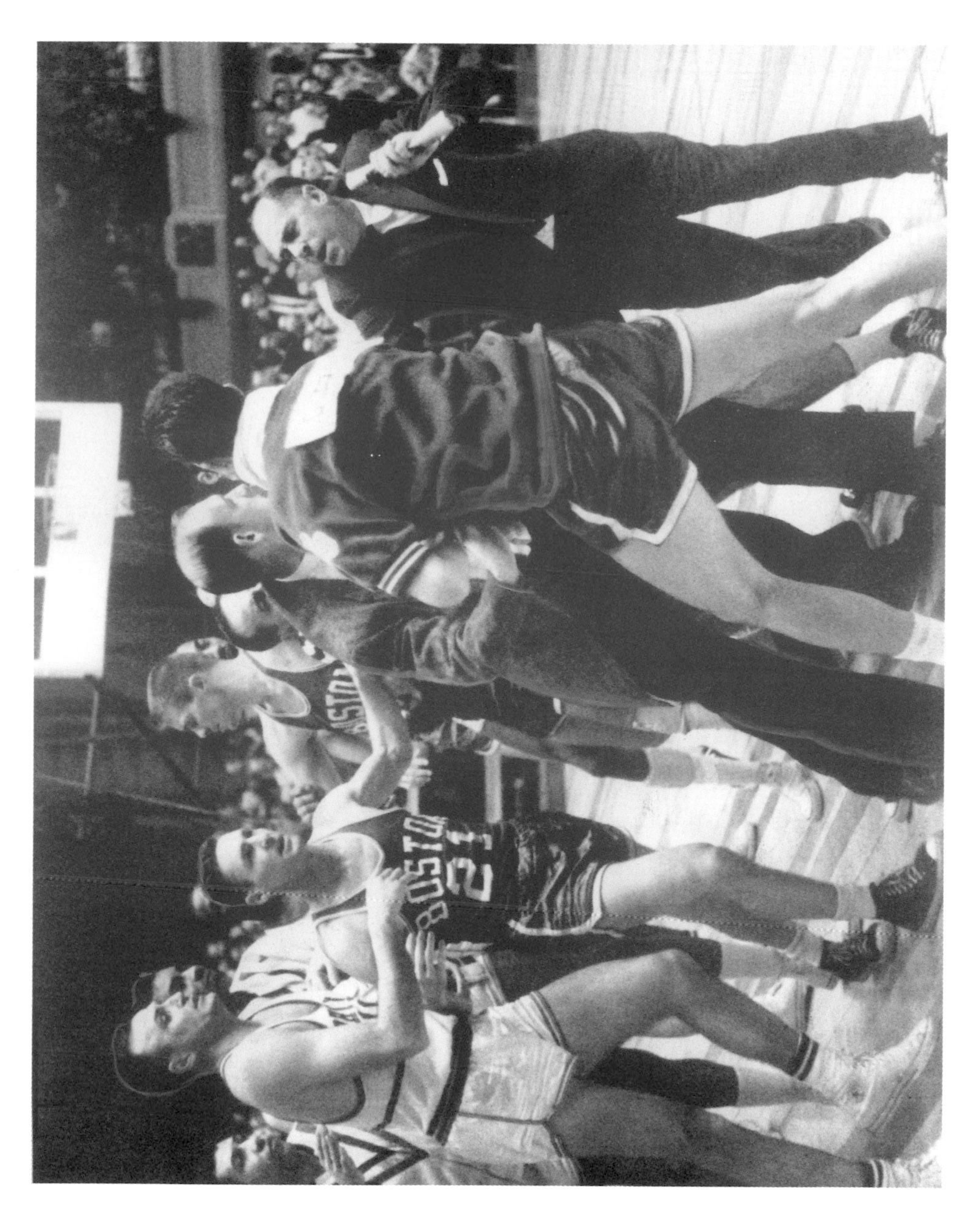

Neal Johnston and Red Auerbach have a disagreement at Convention Hall on January 15, 1960. (Temple University Urban Archives)

During his third year with the Warriors in 1961-62, Chamberlain averaged over 50 points per game and 25 rebounds per contest. (Temple University Urban Archives)

All pro runner Timmy Brown was considered to be one of the most versatile players to ever wear an Eagles uniform. He was also an accomplished hoopster and was drafted by the Warriors in 1959. Ironically, the night Wilt scored 100 points in Hershey, Brown was there and led the Philadelphia Eagles to victory over the Baltimore Colts in the preliminary basketball game.

Wilt Chamberlain, Paul Arizin and Tom Gola converge on Larry Costello as they sweep the Syracuse Nationals in the 1962 Eastern Division semifinals. One year later, the Warriors were playing in San Francisco and the Syracuse Nationals became the Philadelphia 76ers. (Temple University Urban Archives)

Wilt vs. Bill Russell in the 1962 Eastern Division play-offs. Russell was a great rebounder and defensive player, but Wilt was an offensive machine and virtually unstoppable. (Temple University Urban Archives)

From Stephanie Arizin, Wilt found out, you're never too old to learn and never too young to teach.

Wilt in West Philadelphia on an August afternoon.

Eddie Gottlieb, "the mogul of basketball." (Temple University Urban Archives)

1947 SPHAS Jersey (Replica)
(NBA Hardwood Classics)
Offered by Mitchell and Ness Nostalgia Co., 1229 Walnut Street, Philadelphia, PA 19107

1959 Philadelphia Warriors Jersey (Replica)
(NBA Hardwood Classics)
Offered by Mitchell and Ness Nostalgia Co., 1229 Walnut Street, Philadelphia, PA 19107

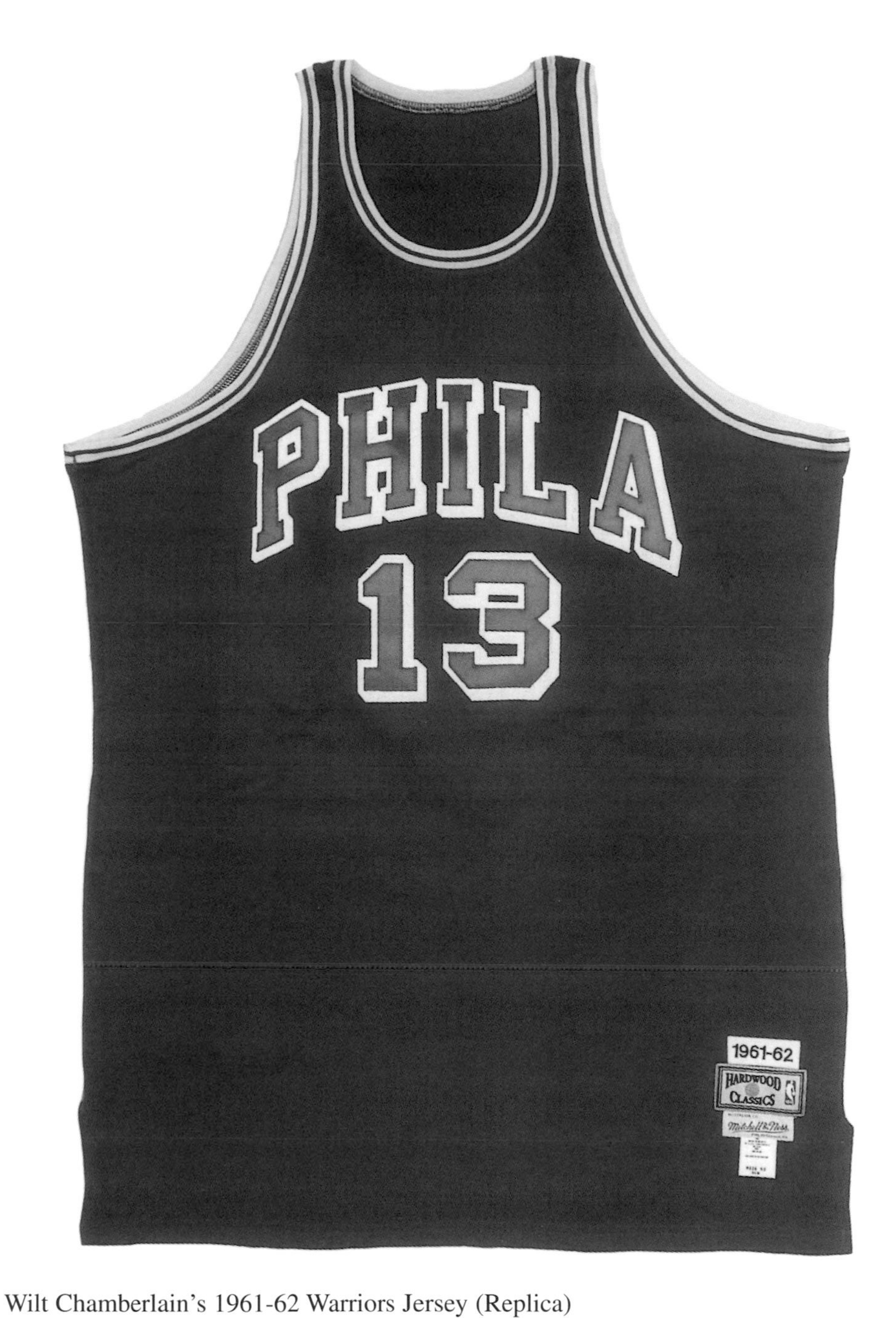

Wilt Chamberlain's 1961-62 Warriors Jersey (Replica)
(NBA Hardwood Classics)
Offered by Mitchell and Ness Nostalgia Co., 1229 Walnut Street, Philadelphia, PA 19107

SPHAS

PLAYERS ROSTER

1918-26

(Partial Listing)

Player	Position	Place of Origin
Davey Banks	Guard	New York
Edwin “Hughie” Black	Guard	Philadelphia
Mark “Mockie” Bunin	Forward-Center	Philadelphia
Eddie Gottlieb	Guard	Philadelphia
Babe Klotz	Center	New York
Stretch Meehan	Center	New York
Charlie Neuman	Forward	Philadelphia
Harry Passon	Guard-Forward	Philadelphia
Chicky Passon	Forward	Philadelphia
Lou Schneiderman	Forward-Center	Philadelphia
Charles Tettemer	Forward	Trenton

SPHAS

PLAYERS ROSTER

Eastern League (1929-32)

American Basketball League (1933-49)

Player	Position	Seasons	College
Oscar Baldwin	Forward	1947-48	Muhlenberg
Moe Becker	Forward	1943-44	Duquesne
Mike Bloom	Center	1938-39	Temple
Si Boardman	Forward	1939-40	NYU
Stan Brown	Forward	1946-49	None
Irv Davis	Forward	1941-47	CCNY
Gil Fitch	Forward	1932-39	Temple
Jerry Fleishman	Guard	1943-46	NYU
Lou Forman	Center	1930-34	Dickinson
Dave Fox	Forward	1948-49	Temple
Mooney Freemark	Guard	1946-47	None
Dutch Garfinkle	Forward	1944-46	St. Johns
Gorham Getchell	Center	1948-49	Temple
Ben Goldfadden	Center	1942-43	CCNY
Moe Goldman	Center	1934-43	CCNY
Shikey Gotthofer	Forward	1933-43	None
Leo Gottlieb	Guard	1939-40	None
Matt Guokas	Forward	1945-46	St. Joseph's
Jack Hewson	Center	1946-47	Temple
Art Hillhouse	Center	1943-46	LIU
Ralph Kaplowitz	Guard	1945-46	NYU
Cy Kaselman	Forward	1929-42	None
Red Klotz	Guard	1942-48	Villanova
Herman Knuppel	Center	1943-44	Panzer
Inky Lautman	Guard	1933-47	None
Babe Liman	Center-Forward	1929-32	None
Harry Litwack	Guard	1930-36	Temple
Eddie Lyons	Guard	1947-49	Temple
Chink Morganstine	Forward	1941-45	Temple
Elmore Morganthaler	Center	1947-49	New Mexico

SPHAS
Players Roster (Cont'd)

Player	Position	Seasons	College
Bill McCahan	Forward	1948-49	Duke
Charlie Mosicant	Center	1941-42	None
Bernie Opper	Guard	1945-47	Kentucky
Howie Radar	Forward	1944-45	LIU
Len Radar	Forward	1944-45	LIU
Ash Resnick	Forward	1938-39	None
Red Rosan	Forward	1936-43	Temple
Petey Rosenberg	Guard	1938-46	St. Joseph's
Irv Rothenberg	Center	1944-45	LIU
Ozzie Schectman	Guard	1941-46	LIU
Butch Schwartz	Forward	1941-48	LIU
George Senesky	Guard	1945-46	St. Joseph's
Red Sherr	Center	1929-32	Penn
Mendy Snyder	Guard	1946-48	Temple
Frank Stanczak	Guard	1948-49	None
Aaron Tanitsky	Forward	1947-49	Penn
Irv Torgoff	Forward	1940-44	LIU
Len Weiner	Forward	1946-49	None
Yock Welsh	Guard	1929-31	None
Red Wolfe	Forward	1933-43	St. John's
Bill Zubic	Forward	1948-49	None

SPHAS

PLAYERS ROSTER

As an Exhibition Team

1949-54

(Partial Listing)

Paul Brandenburg	Guard-Forward	North Carolina
Tom Brennan	Forward	Villanova
Stan Brown	Forward	None
Charlie Burns	Guard	None
George Dempsey	Guard	Kings College
Al Ingber	Guard	PMC
Bob Lojewski	Forward	Temple
Pete Monska	Forward	Westchester State
Izzy Osherow	Guard	Westchester State
Bob Peterson	Center	None
Jack Stein	Forward	None

PHILADELPHIA WARRIORS

PLAYERS ROSTER

1946-62

Player	Position	Seasons Played	College
Paul Arizin	Forward	1950-52, 54-62	Villanova
Robert Armstrong	Forward	1956-57	Mich. State
Alvin Attles	Guard	1960-62	N.Car. A&T
Ernie Beck	Guard	1953-54, 55-60	Penn
Hank Beenders	Forward	1947-48	LIU
Nelson Bobb	Guard	1949-53	Temple
Jake Bornheimer	Forward	1948-50	Muhlenberg
Costic Borsavage	Forward-Ctr.	1950-51	Temple
Walter Budko	Forward	1951-52	Columbia
Bill Closs	Forward	1950-51	Rice
Ed Conlin	Forward	1960-62	Fordham
Larry Costello	Guard	1954-55, 56-57	Niagara
Chink Crossin	Guard	1947-50	Penn
Wilt Chamberlain	Center	1959-62	Kansas
Howie Dallmar	Forward	1946-49	Penn/Stanfd.
Walter Davis	Center	1953-58	Texas A&M
George Dempsey	Guard	1954-58	Kings (Del.)
Patrick Dunn	Guard	1957-58	Utah State
Phillip Farbman	Guard	1948-49	CCNY
Danny Finn	Guard	1952-55	St. John's
Jerry Fleishman	Guard	1946-50, 52-53	NYU
Joe Fulks	Forward	1946-54	Murray State
Vern Gardner	Forward	1949-52	Wyoming
Jack George	Guard	1953-58	LaSalle
Tom Gola	Guard	1955-56, 57-62	LaSalle
Joe Graboski	Forward	1953-61	None
Norman Grekin	Forward	1953-54	LaSalle
Matt Guokas	Forward-Ctr.	1946-47	St. Joseph's
Chuck Halbert	Center	1947-48	W. Texas St.
Vern Hatton	Guard	1958-61	Kentucky
Larry Hennessy	Guard	1955-56	LaSalle
Art Hillhouse	Center	1946-48	LIU
Andy Johnson	Forward	1958-61	Portland

Philadelphia Warriors
Players Roster, 1946-62
(Cont'd)

Neil Johnston	Center	1951-59	Ohio State
Fred Kadelka	Guard	1952-53	Chicago
Ralph Kaplowitz	Guard	1946-48	NYU
Michael Kerns	Guard	1954-55	Princeton
Bill Kennedy	Guard	1960-61	Temple
York Larese	Guard	1961-62	No. Carolina
Hal Lear	Guard	1957-58	Temple
Fred Lewis	Guard	1949-50	LIU
Ted Luckenbill	Forward	1961-62	Houston
Jack McCloskey	Guard	1952-53	Penn
Robert McNeil	Guard	1961-62	St. Joseph's
Tom Meschery	Forward	1961-62	St. Mary's
Ed Mikan	Center	1951-52	DePaul
Bill Mlkvy	Guard	1952-53	Temple
Leo Mogus	Forward	1949-51	Youngstown
John Murphy	Guard	1946-47	None
Jim Mooney	Forward	1952-53	Villanova
Jackie Moore	Forward	1955-57	LaSalle
Elmo Morganthaler	Center	1948-49	New Mexico
Angelo Musi	Guard	1946-49	Temple
Jim Nolan	Forward	1949-50	GA Tech
Robert O'Brien	Forward	1947-48	Kansas
Claude Overton	Guard	1952-53	E. Cent. OK
Easy Parham	Guard	1950-51	Tex.Wesleyan
Chuck Parsley	Guard	1949-50	Western KY
John Payak	Forward	1949-50	Bowling Gr.
Melvin Payton	Guard	1951-52	Tulane
Jim Phelan	Guard	1953-54	LaSalle
Andy Phillip	Guard	1950-52	Illinois
Ralph Polson	Forward	1952-53	Whitworth
Frank Radovich	Forward	1961-62	Indiana
George Radovich	Guard	1952-53	Wyoming
Ray Radziszewski	Forward	1957-58	St. Joseph's
Jack Rocker	Forward	1947-48	Cal.Berkeley
Guy Rodgers	Guard	1958-62	Temple

Philadelphia Warriors
Players Roster, 1946-62
(Cont'd)

Petey Rosenberg	Guard	1946-47	St. Joseph's
Lenny Rosenbluth	Forward	1957-59	No.Carolina
Joe Ruklick	Center	1959-62	Northwestern
Jerry Rullo	Guard	1946-47, 48-50	Temple
Ed Sadowski	Center	1948-50	Seton Hall
Woody Sauldsberry	Forward	1957-60	Texas South.
Robert Schafer	Guard	1955-56	Villanova
George Senesky	Guard	1946-54	St. Joseph's
Fred Sheffield	Forward	1946-47	Utah
Gene Shue	Guard	1954-55	Maryland
Guy Sparrow	Forward	1959-60	Detroit
Irv Torgoff	Forward	1948-49	LIU
Paul Walther	Guard	1953-54	Tennessee
Mark Workman	Forward	1952-53	W. Virginia
Robert Zawoluk	Forward	1953-55	St. John's

BASKETBALL ASSOCIATION OF AMERICA 1946-47

EASTERN DIVISION	W	L
Washington Capitols	49	11
Philadelphia Warriors	35	25
New York Knickerbockers	33	27
Providence Steamrollers	28	32
Toronto Huskies	22	38
Boston Celtics	22	38

WESTERN DIVISION	W	L
Chicago Stags	39	22
St. Louis Bombers	38	23
Cleveland Rebels	30	30
Detroit Falcons	20	40
Pittsburgh Ironmen	15	45

Sixty games were played during the regular season. Joe Fulks won the scoring title with a 23.2 ppg average. In the quarterfinals the Warriors defeated the St. Louis Bombers 2 out of 3, then shut out the New York Knicks 2 to 0 in the semifinals. In the finals, Philadelphia defeated the Chicago Stags in 4 out of 5 games to win the BAA championship.

BASKETBALL ASSOCIATION
OF AMERICA
1947-48

EASTERN DIVISION	W	L
Philadelphia Warriors	27	21
New York Knicks	26	22
Boston Celtics	20	28
Providence Steamrollers	6	42

WESTERN DIVISION	W	L
St. Louis Bombers	29	19
Baltimore Bullets	28	20
Chicago Stags	28	20
Washington Capitols	28	20

Only 48 games were played during the second season, to cut travel expenses. Detroit, Cleveland, Toronto and Pittsburgh dropped out. Washington moved to the Western Division and the Baltimore Bullets (from the American Basketball League) joined the BAA to create two divisions with four teams. The Bullets responded by defeating the Warriors for the championship in 4 out of 6 games.

BASKETBALL ASSOCIATION OF AMERICA

1948-49

EASTERN DIVISION	W	L
Washington Capitols	38	22
New York Knicks	32	28
Baltimore Bullets	29	31
Philadelphia Warriors	28	32
Boston Celtics	25	35
Providence Steamrollers	12	48

WESTERN DIVISION	W	L
Rochester Royals	45	15
Minneapolis Lakers	44	16
Chicago Stags	38	22
St. Louis Bombers	29	31
Fort Wayne Pistons	22	38
Indianapolis Jets	18	42

In the 3rd year of the BAA, the league resumed a 60-game schedule. Washington and Baltimore moved to the Eastern Division. Four teams from the National Basketball League (which operated in the midwest) joined the BAA's Western Division: The Rochester Royals, Minneapolis Lakers, Fort Wayne Pistons, and Indianapolis Jets. The Warriors experienced their first losing season and were eliminated by Washington 2 to 0 in the Eastern Division semifinals. The Lakers defeated the Capitols 4 out of 6 games to win the championship.

NATIONAL BASKETBALL ASSOCIATION

1949-50

EASTERN DIVISION	W	L
Syracuse Nationals	51	13
New York Knicks	40	28
Washington Capitols	32	36
Philadelphia Warriors	26	42
Baltimore Bullets	25	43
Boston Celtics	22	46

CENTRAL DIVISION	W	L
Minneapolis Lakers	51	17
Rochester Royals	51	17
Fort Wayne Pistons	40	28
Chicago Stags	40	28
St. Louis Bombers	26	42

WESTERN DIVISION	W	L
Indianapolis Olympians	39	25
Anderson Packers	37	27
Tri-Cities Blackhawks	29	35
Sheboygan Redskins	22	40
Waterloo Hawks	19	43
Denver Nuggets	11	51

The Providence Steamrollers and Indianapolis Jets folded. The six remaining teams from the National Basketball League: the Syracuse Nationals, Anderson Packers, Tri-Cities Blackhawks, Sheboygan Redskins, Waterloo Hawks and Denver Nuggets, along with the new Indianapolis Olympians joined the BAA and the league was renamed the National Basketball Association. There were 17 teams, and the league was divided into three divisions. In a complicated play-off scheme, the Minneapolis Lakers defeated the Syracuse Nationals to win the title.

NATIONAL BASKETBALL ASSOCIATION

1950-51

EASTERN DIVISION	W	L
Philadelphia Warriors	40	26
Boston Celtics	39	30
New York Knicks	36	30
Syracuse Nationals	32	34
Baltimore Bullets	24	42
Washington Capitols	10	25

WESTERN DIVISION	W	L
Minneapolis Lakers	44	24
Rochester Royals	41	27
Fort Wayne Pistons	32	36
Indianapolis Olympians	31	37
Tri-Cities Blackhawks	25	43

The NBA lost 7 teams, Washington dropped out after 35 games, and the league was left with a more streamlined 10 teams in two divisions. Philadelphia won the Eastern Division, but lost to Syracuse 2-0 in the play-offs. In the finals, the Rochester Royals defeated the New York Knicks in a 7-game series.

NATIONAL BASKETBALL ASSOCIATION

1951-52

EASTERN DIVISION	W	L
Syracuse Nationals	40	26
Boston Celtics	39	27
New York Knicks	37	29
Philadelphia Warriors	33	33
Baltimore Bullets	20	46

WESTERN DIVISION	W	L
Rochester Royals	41	25
Minneapolis Lakers	40	26
Indianapolis Olympians	34	32
Fort Wayne Pistons	29	37
Milwaukee Hawks	17	49

The Tri-Cities Blackhawks (who played their games in 3 cities) became the Milwaukee Hawks. All ten teams in the league played 66 games. Paul Arizin won the scoring title, but Philadelphia finished in 4th place with a 33-33 record, and lost again to the Syracuse Nationals in the semifinals. The New York Knicks again reached the finals, but the Minneapolis Lakers won the title in seven games.

NATIONAL BASKETBALL ASSOCIATION

1952-53

EASTERN DIVISION	W	L
New York Knicks	47	23
Syracuse Nationals	47	24
Boston Celtics	46	25
Baltimore Bullets	16	54
Philadelphia Warriors	12	57

WESTERN DIVISION	W	L
Minneapolis Lakers	48	22
Rochester Royals	44	26
Fort Wayne Pistons	36	33
Indianapolis Olympians	28	43
Milwaukee Hawks	27	44

The league played 69-71 games. Center Neil Johnston won the first of three consecutive scoring titles, but the Philadelphia Warriors won only 12 games. The New York Knicks and Minneapolis Lakers again met in the finals and the Lakers won their second straight championship behind George Mikan, Jim Pollard and Vern Mikkelsen.

NATIONAL BASKETBALL ASSOCIATION

1953-54

EASTERN DIVISION	W	L
New York Knicks	44	28
Boston Celtics	42	30
Syracuse Nationals	42	30
Philadelphia Warriors	29	43
Baltimore Bullets	16	56

WESTERN DIVISION	W	L
Minneapolis Lakers	46	26
Rochester Royals	44	28
Fort Wayne Pistons	40	32
Milwaukee Hawks	21	51

The Indianapolis Olympians disbanded leaving the league with 9 teams in two divisions. The league played 72 games. The Warriors experienced their second losing season and finished in 4th place. The Minneapolis Lakers defeated the Syracuse Nationals in 7 games to win their fourth NBA title, and what would be their last championship in Minneapolis.

NATIONAL BASKETBALL ASSOCIATION

1954-55

EASTERN DIVISION	W	L
Syracuse Nationals	43	29
New York Knicks	38	34
Boston Celtics	36	36
Philadelphia Warriors	33	39
Baltimore Bullets	3	11

WESTERN DIVISION	W	L
Fort Wayne Pistons	43	29
Minneapolis Lakers	40	32
Rochester Royals	29	43
Milwaukee Hawks	26	46

The Baltimore Bullets dropped out after playing 14 games leaving the league with 8 teams. Paul Arizin returned to the NBA after two years in the Marines, and averaged 21 points per game. The Syracuse Nationals won the championship, defeating the Fort Wayne Pistons in 7 games.

NATIONAL BASKETBALL ASSOCIATION

1955-56

EASTERN DIVISION	W	L
Philadelphia Warriors	45	27
Boston Celtics	39	33
Syracuse Nationals	35	37
New York Knicks	35	37

WESTERN DIVISION	W	L
Fort Wayne Pistons	37	35
Minneapolis Lakers	33	39
St. Louis Hawks	33	39
Rochester Royals	31	41

The Milwaukee Hawks moved to St. Louis. The Philadelphia Warriors won the Eastern Division title, then defeated the Fort Wayne Pistons for the championship in 5 games, behind the play of Neil Johnston, Paul Arizin, and rookie Tom Gola from LaSalle College.

NATIONAL BASKETBALL ASSOCIATION

1956-57

EASTERN DIVISION	W	L
Boston Celtics	44	28
Syracuse Nationals	38	34
Philadelphia Warriors	37	35
New York Knicks	36	36

WESTERN DIVISION	W	L
St. Louis Hawks	34	38
Minneapolis Lakers	34	38
Fort Wayne Pistons	34	38
Rochester Royals	31	41

The Boston Celtics acquired Bill Russell from St. Louis, drafted Tom Heinsohn from Holy Cross, and began a dynasty that would last until the late '60s. Philadelphia lost Tom Gola to the army, finished in third place, and lost to Syracuse in the semifinals. In the championship series, Boston beat St. Louis to earn their first NBA title.

NATIONAL BASKETBALL ASSOCIATION

1957-58

EASTERN DIVISION	W	L
Boston Celtics	49	23
Syracuse Nationals	41	31
Philadelphia Warriors	37	35
New York Knicks	35	37

WESTERN DIVISION	W	L
St. Louis Hawks	41	31
Detroit Pistons	33	39
Cincinnati Royals	33	39
Minneapolis Lakers	19	53

The Fort Wayne Pistons moved to Detroit, and the Rochester Royals went to Cincinnati. Philadelphia finished third again with the same record of 37-35, but this time they defeated Syracuse in the first round, and met Boston in the Eastern Division finals. The Celtics won in 5, then lost to the St. Louis Hawks in a six-game championship series.

NATIONAL BASKETBALL ASSOCIATION

1958-59

EASTERN DIVISION	W	L
Boston Celtics	52	20
New York Knicks	40	32
Syracuse Nationals	35	37
Philadelphia Warriors	32	40

WESTERN DIVISION	W	L
St. Louis Hawks	49	23
Minneapolis Lakers	33	39
Detroit Pistons	28	44
Cincinnati Royals	19	53

With nagging injuries to Paul Arizin and Neil Johnston (who sat out most of the season), the Warriors finished fourth in the division and out of thc play-offs. The Boston Celtics beat the Minneapolis Lakers for the title.

NATIONAL BASKETBALL ASSOCIATION

1959-60

EASTERN DIVISION	W	L
Boston Celtics	59	16
Philadelphia Warriors	49	26
Syracuse Nationals	45	30
New York Knicks	27	48

WESTERN DIVISION	W	L
St. Louis Hawks	46	29
Detroit Pistons	30	45
Minneapolis Lakers	25	50
Cincinnati Royals	19	56

The league increased their schedule to 75 games. Boston won a record 59 games but felt some heat from Philadelphia. Wilt Chamberlain arrived after playing one year with the Harlem Globetrotters, and led the NBA in scoring and rebounding. Philadelphia won 17 more games than the previous year and trounced the Syracuse Nationals in the Eastern Division semi-finals. In the Eastern finals, the new-look Warriors held their own against the Celtics until Wilt broke his hand in a fight with Tom Heinsohn. Boston won the series in six games, then beat the St. Louis Hawks for their third NBA title.

NATIONAL BASKETBALL ASSOCIATION

1960-61

EASTERN DIVISION	W	L
Boston Celtics	57	22
Philadelphia Warriors	46	33
Syracuse Nationals	38	41
New York Knicks	21	58

WESTERN DIVISION	W	L
St. Louis Hawks	51	28
Los Angeles Lakers	36	43
Detroit Pistons	34	45
Cincinnati Royals	33	46

The Minneapolis Lakers moved to Los Angeles and the season increased to 79 games. Philadelphia won 46 games and finished second to Boston, but were swept by Syracuse in the semifinals. The Celtics met the Hawks again and defeated St. Louis in five games for their fourth NBA title.

NATIONAL BASKETBALL ASSOCIATION

1961-62

EASTERN DIVISION	W	L
Boston Celtics	60	20
Philadelphia Warriors	49	31
Syracuse Nationals	41	39
New York Knicks	29	51

WESTERN DIVISION	W	L
Los Angeles Lakers	54	26
Cincinnati Royals	43	37
Detroit Pistons	37	43
St. Louis Hawks	29	51
Chicago Packers	18	62

The Chicago Packers joined the league as an expansion team, and the NBA played an 80-game schedule. Wilt Chamberlain averaged 50 points per game and on March 2, 1962, scored 100 points against the Knicks in Hershey. The Warriors won 49 games, beat the Syracuse Nationals in the semifinals, and battled the Celtics in the Eastern Division finals. Tied at 3 games apiece, the 7th game was tied when Boston won by two points on a controversial goal-tending call. The Celtics advanced to the finals and defeated the Los Angeles Lakers.